A Word From the Editor

I remember the first time I felt it. I was five years old. The church we attended started a kindergarten, and my closest friends—a set of twins and another little girl—began attending. For whatever reason, my parents opted not to enroll me, and I didn't understand why. I felt left out. My friends were part of something from which I was excluded, and I felt that distinction deeply.

It starts early in life—that feeling that we sometimes get that tells us we don't quite fit in. It grows as we reach middle school, where groups gather and cliques form to let us know who's in and who's not. By the time we reach high school, divisions are crystal clear, even dictating where we can sit to eat our lunch and with whom.

Psychologists have long recognized the need to belong as one of our basic human needs, a major source of human motivation. Their pronouncement, of course, was no surprise to God. The need and the capacity to belong is in our DNA. God created us for relationship. At Creation, God said, "It's not good that the human is alone" (Genesis 2:18). And the rest of the biblical narrative shows us, among many other things, precisely how much we need God and one another and just how interconnected we are, not just to those who live in our present space and time, but to those across time, throughout all generations. We belong to God, and we belong to one another.

The psalmist expressed it beautifully: "Know that the LORD is God—he made us; we belong to him. We are his people, the sheep of his own pasture" (Psalm 100:3). God through the prophet Isaiah declared, "Don't fear, for I have redeemed you; I have called you by name; you are mine. . . . Because you are precious in my eyes, you are honored, and I love you" (Isaiah 43:1, 4).

One of the biggest draws of the early church was the feeling of belonging it offered. Distinctions of class, race, gender, income, and education didn't matter. In Christ's church, everyone was welcomed. Everyone had a place at the table. What mattered—what distinguished this newly emerging faith community—was love, love for God and love for one another.

Nothing was more important, Jesus said. *"You must love the Lord your God with all your heart, with all your being*, and with all your mind. This is the first and greatest commandment. And the second is like it: *You must love your neighbor as you love yourself"* (Matthew 22:37-39). That love—God's love for us, our love for God, and our love for one another—pulls us into community and propels us out, extending the invitation to belong to everyone.

Our readings this quarter assure us that we belong. We belong to God, and we belong to one another. Those on the outside belong to God and to us, too, whether they know it and feel it or not. All it takes is an invitation to the table, a table that belongs not to us, but to Christ.

"There is neither Jew nor Greek; there is neither slave nor free; nor is there male and female, for you are all one in Christ Jesus" (Galatians 3:28).

Jan Turrentine

Jan Turrentine
Editor

Our Writers for This Quarter

Taylor Mills

Taylor Mills is a United Methodist pastor originally from Raleigh, North Carolina. He received a degree in communication from Appalachian State University and a master of divinity degree from Duke Divinity School. He has led churches in Williamston, Raleigh, and Durham, North Carolina. Currently, he is the pastor of Ann Street United Methodist Church in Beaufort, North Carolina.

Taylor's wife, Betsy, works in the school system. Together they try to keep up with their two teenage daughters.

Sue Mink

Sue Mink is a graduate of Wesley Theological Seminary and Carnegie-Mellon University and has her home near Charlottesville, Virginia, but she's often not there! She and her husband, Allan, a retired Air Force officer, have arranged their lives so that they can work entirely online. With that flexibility, they live in other cities around the world for three-month time blocks twice a year. In the past few years, they've lived in Florence, Italy; York, England; Krakow, Poland; Bocas del Toro, Panama; Barcelona, Spain; and Taipei, Taiwan, with many more places planned to visit.

Along with traveling and learning the cultures of her temporary homes, Sue's interests include art, weaving, scuba diving, and learning to cook world cuisines. Sue and her husband have two adult children, Jessica and Rob, and one grandson. Sue's been writing for Cokesbury for over a decade and loves studying and researching God's Word.

Greg Weeks

Greg Weeks is a retired elder in The United Methodist Church. He pastored congregations in the Missouri area before retiring in 2019 after 43 years of service. An important part of his ministry was writing curriculum and other material for The United Methodist Publishing House. He is the author of the Job volume for the Abingdon Basic Bible Commentary series.

Greg lives in the St. Louis area with his wife, Barbara. They have two young adult children, Cameron and Emma. He continues writing in retirement, serving as a "Faith Perspectives" columnist for *The St. Louis Post-Dispatch*. He also writes a blog titled "Being Christian Without Losing Your Mind."

Introduction to the Study

What is the true meaning and purpose of the church? We might have had an easier answer just a short time ago, but we've had to reexamine this in the past year with the outbreak of COVID-19. We have not been able to gather in our buildings and worship together physically. In many instances, it has been difficult to be a community when we can't meet face-to-face.

I've spoken with some people who have been afraid that their church will not survive. But many of my pastor friends have told me that there is a new vibrance and connection within their congregations as they respond to one another's needs and the needs of the community in innovative ways. My church has held food drives; made masks; helped families teach their children; and delivered items to older, at-risk members.

In some ways, church has become more accessible. Shut-ins can worship online with the rest of the community; and for many congregations, the attendance for Bible studies—now held online—has never been higher. I have been worshiping not only with my local congregation, but I am deeply grateful that I was invited to worship online with another congregation, one whose members are, for the most part, ethnically different from me and who meet hundreds of miles from my home. I've been warmly welcomed into this community of Christ and have been graciously given an insight to their hopes, joys, fears, and difficulties during this pandemic.

All these things have opened up a new understanding of my faith and our responsibilities to one another as followers of Jesus Christ. These experiences have reminded us all that the church is not a building, but a community of Christian believers who reach across boundaries of distance, economics, race, and culture.

The Greek word for "church" is *ekklesia*, which means "called out." The first set of readings this quarter explores who God invites into this community and, by extension, whom we should welcome into our faith community as well. The church calls for us to practice radical hospitality, accepting all who answer the call of Christ.

It also reminds us to celebrate our own acceptance into the family of God, realizing that, despite our failings, we too, as sinners, are welcome. Because we are the grateful recipients of radical hospitality, it's something we are blessed to offer to others.

The second group of readings examines how this community of people is bound together and what makes the community work. Christ welcomed the outcast, the alien, sinners, and the poor; but the early church sometimes had difficulties combining all these disparate people into a harmonious whole.

How can each person bring his or her specific gifts to the service of the church? How can the church discern the will of God in worship, service to one another, and in disagreements? How can a church remain vibrant, and what does God expect of this community? These readings refocus our commitment as a church to God and to one another by examining spiritual discernment, spiritual renewal, and our covenant relationship with Christ.

During the pandemic, some churches have had a difficult time knowing their purpose and mission and surviving while unable to meet in-person. Perhaps their focus has been drifting away from God's desires, and the call to spiritual growth and service in these Scriptures can help them redefine a path to vibrant worship and service, even among challenging restrictions and restructuring.

The third set of readings this quarter examines fellowship together, specifically fellowship focused on sharing food. Because food nourishes us, it's an apt symbol for the strength and nourishment we receive through faith and fellowship.

Jesus often ate with outcasts as a way of inviting them into his community of believers. One of his final acts before his crucifixion was to symbolically offer his body and blood as a way of strengthening the faith of his disciples.

Believers look forward to a heavenly banquet where all will be gathered to feast with the Lord. These readings explore how we as a church can feed the bodies and souls of others. This is the way we become Christ to the world, and so it is an integral call of his people.

This has been a challenging time for the church, but it has also given us a chance to reexamine our purpose, our goals, and our service to one another. As God's holy people striving for a dynamic relationship with the Lord, we can only expect this sacred community to be ever-changing and adapting to the needs of the world around us as we listen to God's direction.

If there's one thing that characterizes a dying church, it's resistance to change and complacency. The look and structure of the church has evolved throughout the centuries, but the spirit of a vibrant and obedient faith community has not. It has always been characterized by the words of the *Shema* in Deuteronomy 6:5: "Love the LORD your God with all your heart, all your being, and all your strength." And as Jesus added, "And the second is like it: *You must love your neighbor as you love yourself*" (Matthew 22:39; Mark 12:31; Luke 10:27).

May we continue to grow in faith, in fellowship, and in service, working with the guidance of the Lord to find new ways to reach those who do not yet know us and better serve and nourish those who do.

Leviticus 19:33-34; 24:22

Strangers Yourselves

Should immigrants enjoy the same protections under the law?

At one time or another, all of us have felt that we didn't quite fit in. Maybe it was a social group, an organization, or even a family. We've all had the experience of feeling like an outsider.

Foreign travel reminds me of how it feels to be an outsider. I haven't traveled as much as I would like to. (Who has?) But even when I visit a domestic city for the first time, I realize how dependent I am on others. These days, I have GPS to help me; but I remember depending on maps and directions from gas station attendants.

Some people get in trouble in new places because they don't know all the local laws or customs. I got a warning ticket one time, for example, because I didn't know that the town I was visiting prohibited drivers from passing on the right. How was I to know?

In Leviticus 24:22, we read that the Lord's law is to be applied equally to "immigrant or citizen alike." Just because someone is from elsewhere, he or she is still subject to the law. But that runs both ways. The immigrant is also protected by that same law. God doesn't have one set of laws for immigrants and one set of laws for citizens.

This probably seemed unfair to some citizens. Why should they have to give immigrants the protections of the law? They weren't part of the "in group." They weren't "from around here." Maybe the immigrants paid taxes (for using roads, for example), but they weren't citizens.

Certainly, some must have thought, citizens should enjoy some privileges.

But the way God saw it, the Israelites needed to understand what it was like to be immigrants because they were once immigrants. Remember that? God said, "You were immigrants in the land of Egypt." Therefore, "when immigrants live in your land with you, you must not cheat them" (Leviticus 19:33, 34).

God encouraged the Israelites and all of us to have empathy for immigrants because we have all been immigrants in one way or another. We have all just been passing through here or there. Even a person who has never gone more than a few miles from home has known the universal human feeling of being a stranger in one way or another.

The Law, God said, will apply to immigrants and citizens alike because that is justice, but also because that will remind us that we are all strangers in some sense. In a way, God is the only one who fully belongs. We humans are part of God's world, not owners of God's world.

God's law treats immigrants and citizens alike because both are precious to God. As the psalmist wrote, "The earth is the LORD's and everything in it, the world and its inhabitants too" (Psalm 24:1). So it stands to reason that God would say, "Any immigrant who lives with you must be treated as if they were one of your citizens" (Leviticus 19:34).

God of us all, thank you for giving all of us protection under your law. Amen.

Acts 16:13-15

Gentile Hospitality

How does our relationship in Jesus bind us to Christians from other places?

In the spring of 1996, I joined several friends from our Wesley Foundation College Campus Ministry on a trip to Monterrey, Mexico, and the surrounding area. We visited the seminarians of the Seminario Metodista Juan Wesley. At least one night during our trip, we were guests in the homes of local church members. I remember vividly how gracious and hospitable my hosts were.

They had little compared to my comforts back home. They carried their own bucket of water to flush the toilet. There was no hot water for the shower. Though they had so little, they did everything they could to make me feel welcome. They served foods to us that they did not typically enjoy themselves. One even gave me his personal Bible in Spanish, which I treasure today.

I was the stranger in their midst. I was the outsider, the alien. They owed me nothing, but they gave of what little they had to make me feel welcomed. In this way, they showed us what love looks like. They honored the biblical model of welcoming the stranger and showing hospitality to the visitor in your midst.

Luke writes of similar experiences outside the city gate of Philippi. He and others were accompanying Paul on missionary journeys. When the sabbath came, they went looking for a place for prayer. It just so happened that a woman there, Lydia, was a "God-worshipper" (Acts 16:14). That was a term Jews used for Gentiles who worshiped and feared Israel's God.

We learn that Lydia was from the city of Thyatira, and she dealt in purple cloth. It is likely that she ran her own small business, as we'd say today. Purple cloth was not easy to come by in those times. Her name, *Lydia*, probably indicates that she was from the Greek region of Lydia in Asia Minor.

As the story goes, Lydia listened to Paul's preaching, and "the Lord enabled her to embrace Paul's message" (verse 14). That is, she received the gospel message about the ministry of Jesus Christ. This led to her baptism and the baptisms of those in her household. They became Christians. Biblical studies and church tradition suggest that Lydia was, then, the first documented European convert.

Once Lydia had received the Lord and her household had been baptized, she extended her hospitality to Paul, Luke, and the others traveling with them. This was not a native Jewish land. The apostles and their companions were the guests, not the hosts. And they were the beneficiaries of Gentile hospitality.

Luke and the others never forgot Lydia's generosity of spirit and her welcome. They memorialized her in Acts 16:11-15. Her hospitality is written into God's Word as an example to us all, whether we are host or guest, of how the gospel of the Lord Jesus binds us together, no matter who we are or where we are from.

Lord Jesus, help me to show hospitality to others as Lydia did for Paul and his companions. Amen.

1

Isaiah 16:1-5

Welcoming the Refugees

How should you act when someone needs refuge?

Some explanation is in order. In Isaiah 15:1–16:14, we read a proclamation concerning Moab, an ancient kingdom in the area of modern-day Jordan. In the Old Testament, the Kingdom of Moab was usually in conflict with Israel.

Before Isaiah's time, Moab was the place where Moses died when he could not enter the Promised Land (Deuteronomy 34:5). After the conquest of Canaan, Israelite relations with the Moabites were mixed. Right after today's text, Isaiah reflects on "Moab's pride" (Isaiah 16:6).

But the start of Isaiah 16 has the Moabites fleeing danger and seeking refuge and justice in Zion (verses 1-4). The attacker must have been a superior military force, but the text does not tell us which one. Verses 4-5 look ahead to a time of peace and justice for the region.

We read today about how "the daughters of Moab at the fords of the Arnon [were] like orphaned birds pushed from the nest" (verse 2). The writer was sympathetic to their plight. Though they had a mixed history with Moab, the writer was concerned for the safety of the Moabite refugees.

The prophet gave these instructions to the Israelite ruler: "Hide the outcasts; keep the fugitives hidden" (verse 3). That is, protect the fugitive Moabites in Israel. "Let the outcasts of Moab live among you. Be a hiding place for them from the destroyer" (verse 4). If the Moabites could be granted resident alien status in Israel, they would be afforded certain protections.

From time to time in our modern world, refugees move across borders seeking protection from their neighbors. This creates tensions between the residents and the newcomers. but it also presents opportunities for healing and new community.

In the prophet's eyes, Israel would be known by how it behaved in Moab's time of need. There were lots of options. The Israelite leader could close the border to the Moabites, leaving them to die at the hands of their attackers. Or if the leader let them cross over, he could take advantage of the vulnerable refugees, possibly forcing them into servitude and/or extorting them for what riches they might provide him. But God would have Israel give the Moabite refugees protection by hiding them and letting them live among the people.

Unfortunately for us, the Bible does not tell us what happened to these particular Moabite refugees on this certain occasion. We do not know if the Israelite ruler afforded them resident alien status. But God conveyed the divine will through the prophet: No matter how relations have been with the Moabites in the past, welcome and protect them in their time of need.

God above, look with compassion on all the refugees of the world, I pray. Amen.

Hospitable Leaders

How does the character of an elder or other leader affect the whole church?

Groups of people—whether in teams, companies, churches, or other kinds of groups—take their cues from their leadership. If the CEO is cutthroat, for example, the corporate culture at that company will follow. If the coach is disrespectful of other teams, the team members will be, too. Sportsmanship will suffer as a result.

The same goes for churches. If the pastor or lay leaders are belligerent, the church will be in constant conflict. If the bishop over more than one church is not a person of good character, the whole body will suffer as a result.

This was true in the early church, and it is still true today. When Paul wrote to Titus, he gave his perspective on how leaders of the church should behave. These elders/overseers/supervisors are "God's managers," he wrote (Titus 1:7). They should be without fault.

That may seem like an unrealistic ideal, but Paul believed it is possible with God's help. "They shouldn't be stubborn, irritable, addicted to alcohol, a bully, or greedy" (verse 7). In some of his other letters, Paul wrote lists of good and bad qualities associated with Christian discipleship.

We have to remember that this was the early church. It was a critical time in the interpretation of what it means to be a follower of Jesus, and it was important to establish standards of behavior. Jesus was not physically walking and talking with his disciples anymore. It was a time in which the Holy Spirit led the apostles and their followers in how to organize themselves.

Perhaps Paul had seen bad examples of leadership before. He referred to how he left Titus behind in Crete so that he could "appoint elders in each city" (verse 5).

Paul told Titus that, instead of being stubborn, irritable, addicted to alcohol, a bully, or greedy, elders "should show hospitality, love what is good, and be reasonable, ethical, godly, and self-controlled" (verse 8).

Take note that hospitality is at the beginning of this list. What would it look like for a bishop to be hospitable? I can't imagine that my United Methodist bishop and her husband are expected to invite the hundreds of pastors under her charge to have dinner at her house. But she shows hospitality in other ways. She is available to us when we need her. She is always approachable in spirit, never intimidating. She prays for us.

And in so doing, she sets the tone for the entire conference of clergy and laity. We are inclined to be hospitable in our churches because we see her example. That goes for all leaders in Paul's early church and in our church today, even churches without bishops. The tone is set in the leadership.

God, grant us hospitable bishops, elders, lay leaders, and Christians in every place. Amen.

God's Presence With Us

Why should you bother being hospitable toward the outsider?

It might be that some followers of the faith consider hospitality to be less important than other virtues. But God's word through Jeremiah is that hospitality is essential. In fact, unless God sees care being taken toward "the immigrant, orphan, or widow," God will not dwell in that place (Jeremiah 7:6-7).

What a startling word! Remember that God had dwelt with Judah through the Temple. But in this text, God makes that presence conditional. The people were not to take it for granted. If they acted contrary to God's ways, God would not dwell with them!

What did it mean that some were taking advantage of the immigrant? From other biblical accounts, we can surmise that some were exploiting the immigrants for labor, money, or other rewards. Sometimes the exploitation was even organized on a corporate or a national level.

I am reminded of efforts in my state to unionize farm workers. Many migrant laborers are not afforded proper protections while they are here planting or picking crops. They are not given safe working conditions that would be guaranteed citizens. If they protest, the employer might threaten to send them back to their home country, even if they are here legally. Why would the employer want to deal with worker complaints when there are waiting lists of other workers who would come here and not complain?

Meanwhile, conditions seldom improve. The only way to make a change in this system is for the employer to feel pressure to change, perhaps by public admonishment (through the media?) or economic pressure (through a boycott?) or some other mechanism.

For Jeremiah, the mechanism of change was God's threat to withdraw the divine presence. There is some suggestion that Jeremiah could have been preaching this sermon in the Temple itself, or at least to people going into the Temple. The first two verses tell him, "Stand near the gate of the Lord's temple and proclaim there this message." So Jeremiah preached to all of "Judah who [entered those] gates to worship the LORD" (verse 2).

The people were not to take false security in their assumption that God's presence is a given. God watched how they treated one another and those from outside the community. The people had taken assurance in the past that, as long as God was in the Temple, the nation would be sustained. But a withdrawal of the divine presence was dangerous to their national and personal security.

Imagine the nations of the world today doing the kind of self-examination for which Jeremiah called. They would do what is right, not just because they were shamed into doing so or because it was economically advantageous. They would be virtuous simply because God expected it of them.

Help me look within, Lord God, and make sure that I am treating others rightly. Amen.

Judged on Our Actions

What are the consequences for not caring for the vulnerable?

Prophets are known for speaking truth to power. In every society, they have emerged to say what needs to be said. A whole section in the middle of the Book of Jeremiah is dedicated to oracles against the kings. As Jeremiah prophesied against the unjust practices in his time, so we today need to look at our leaders and our communities and make sure we are following God's ways, not just our ways.

These prophecies come with negative and positive formulations. There are certain things that should not be done. If they are done, bad things will happen. Conversely, there are virtues for which a people should strive. Where God sees these virtues, God will send blessings. The treatment of immigrants and strangers was part of both formulations in Jeremiah 22:3-5.

First, the negative (what not to do): "Don't exploit or mistreat the refugee, the orphan, and the widow" (Jeremiah 22:3). The one who comes from outside the community seeking safety and refuge is as important as the orphan and the widow. Remember that the social structure and the economy were built around the household. An orphan and a widow would not have had a male head of the household who was responsible for their well-being. Consequently, they were the most vulnerable in that society. The same was true of the refugee.

If the people did not care for the refugee, the orphan, and the widow, then they would fall out of God's favor. The consequence comes in verse 5: "I swear by myself, declares the LORD, that this palace will become a ruin."

Then the positive formulation: "If you obey this command, then through the gates of this palace will come kings who occupy the throne of David, riding on chariots and horses along with their entourage and subjects" (verse 4). What an image! The king of Judah would be given a chain of succession that would be noticed by the other nations for its majesty.

The kings of Judah would be measured by how they treated the vulnerable populations in their midst. If they would keep their part of the covenantal relationship, God would favor them.

We may not live in a time of kings such as that, but those of us in democratic societies locate the power in the people. This also puts the responsibility with the people. God looks upon how we treat the vulnerable people in our midst. God cares about them, and there are consequences for our decisions: negative consequences for mistreatment and positive consequences for beneficence.

As God has said, "Do what is just and right; rescue the oppressed from the power of the oppressor. Don't exploit or mistreat the refugee, the orphan, and the widow" (verse 3).

Call me to account, Lord God, for how I treat the most vulnerable in our midst. Amen.

5

Jeremiah 29:1-23

Being Faithful Captives

How should you act if you must endure through a hard time?

The Babylonian captivity was a terrible time for Israel. The people had been carried off by the forces of Nebuchadnezzar and resettled in a land that was not their own. They were foreigners.

Just as the prophet Jeremiah had spoken about how God's people ought to treat the immigrants and strangers in their midst, so now he wrote to the covenant people who were the immigrants and strangers themselves. Their roles had been reversed.

How would Israel act in this new place? Would they make the best of it? Would they resist? In this letter from God, through Jeremiah, the people were told: "Build houses and settle down; cultivate gardens and eat what they produce. Get married and have children" (Jeremiah 29:5-6).

Furthermore, they were not to wish ill on their captors. They were to "promote the welfare of the city" where God had sent them into exile. They were to "pray to the LORD for it, because [their] future [depended] on its welfare" (verse 7).

This is a bold word! I don't believe I would be comfortable telling captives to respect their captors and pray for the land of their exile. But this was the Lord's word in a context in which God claimed to have sent the people to Babylon. But God said that when "Babylon's seventy years are up, I will come and fulfill my gracious promise to bring you back to this place" (verse 10).

This is followed by the oft-quoted verse 11, in which God says, "I know the plans I have in mind for you, declares the LORD; they are plans for peace, not disaster, to give you a future filled with hope." It is important that this verse not be taken out of context. It is not a verse about human potential or motivation. It is a word for a people in captivity.

To those who didn't go into exile, the Lord said, "I'm going to send the sword, famine, and disease against them. I will make them like rotten figs that are too spoiled to eat . . . because they wouldn't listen to my words, declares the LORD, which I sent them time and again through my servants the prophets" (verses 17, 19).

God's plans can be difficult for us to comprehend. They can be complicated and situational. But Israel was reminded, and we are reminded, that God has our best in mind. Even in dire situations, especially in dire situations, God has our best in mind.

This means that, if we find ourselves in adverse circumstances, even captives to a power that does not recognize God's sovereignty, we are to endure with dignity. We are to pray along with God's best plans in all circumstances and places. When the time is right, God will deliver us from turmoil. Even if others do not show us hospitality, we are to keep the commandments and ordinances of the Lord our God, the one who is "the LORD of heavenly forces, the God of Israel" (verse 4).

No matter what I go through, Lord, keep me faithful to your ways. Amen.

6

Genesis 24:22-25

Hospitality Leads to Availability

How can you be more open to God's will in your life?

From time to time, I have the honor of meeting a married couple for the first time. They might be neighbors. They might have come to visit our church. Eventually, we have an opportunity to visit and get to know one another better.

In those visits, I do enjoy asking them, "So how did you two meet?" Invariably, the couple looks at one another, smiles across their faces, and they delight in telling me the story.

Some couples met through intentional dating opportunities. Others met by accident. But all these stories have a common theme: a sense of God's providence. In other words, they all have a strong sense that God brought them together.

Today, we find ourselves in the middle of a story about how Abraham sought a wife for his son Isaac after the death of Isaac's mother, Sarah. It's worth reading the entire chapter for the whole story, told in a leisurely and novelistic style.

Abraham had decided to send his servant to a well in "Nahor's city in Aramnaharaim" (Genesis 24:10). He gave instructions to the servant to ask a young woman for water. If the woman gave him water and offered water for his camels, then she must be the one who should marry Isaac.

The servant followed all the instructions. He met Rebekah, "daughter of Bethuel the son of Milcah wife of Nahor" (verse 15), who eagerly gave him water and promptly got water for his camels, too. Her act of hospitality toward the servant impressed him, and he "stood gazing at her, wondering silently if the LORD had made his trip successful or not" (verse 21).

Abraham's servant was pretty sure that Rebekah was the woman who should go back and marry his master's son Isaac. But he couldn't ask her to go back with him until he spoke to her father. First, however, he presented Rebekah with a gold ring and two gold bracelets, indicating Abraham's prosperity (verse 22). Then he asked if Rebekah's household could take him in for the night.

We see another sign of Rebekah's hospitality when she responded, "We have plenty of straw and feed for the camels, and a place to spend the night" (verse 25). At this, the servant gave God thanks for showing him the way to the right young woman and household (verses 26-27). When Rebekah's father and brother saw the gold jewelry and heard the story of how the servant came to find Rebekah, they gave their blessing and sent Rebekah to be Isaac's wife.

This story reminds us that one act of hospitality can open up channels of God's providence. Sometimes we are given clear directions by God, as Abraham received in Genesis 24:6-8. But oftentimes, we have a vaguer sense of God's intentions. We may need to put ourselves in a spiritual place where we can discern God's will more clearly. A sure way to do this, to open our ears and eyes to God's will around us, is to practice hospitality.

Make me available, Lord God, to those around me that I might come to know you through them. Amen.

Hospitality Necessitates Generosity

How can you learn to be generous?

In 2 Corinthians 8:1-15, Paul writes to the church in Corinth to encourage their generosity to a common treasury so as to fund the work of evangelism. He first pointed to the Macedonians as examples, but he made clear to the Corinthians that he was not trying to put them down in the process. He merely wanted to point out how the Macedonians and the Corinthians had found joy in generosity in the past.

Paul anticipated that someone would object and say that, of course, others had given more because they had more. But Paul said that people can only be expected to give in proportion to what they have (2 Corinthians 8:12). The important thing is to give generously, to take joy in giving (as the Macedonians did), and to complete a work of generosity once it has started (verse 11).

The ultimate example of generosity came from Jesus, Paul said. "You know the grace of our Lord Jesus Christ. Although he was rich, he became poor for your sakes, so that you could become rich through his poverty" (verse 9). Jesus was rich, Paul said, in that he left the glory of heaven to walk among us. We're reminded of the hymn to Christ that Paul quoted in Philippians 2:6-8.

As we are looking at hospitality in this collection of readings, today's passage reminds us that hospitality is not only about domestic matters. The way we use our money is a matter of hospitality, too. When we spend our money only on ourselves, we are not eagerly participating in the work of evangelism. To show hospitality, rather, we ought to be generous in giving what God has so generously given us.

The model we see in the letter to the Corinthians, in other places in Paul's letters, and in Acts shows us that churches should give to common ministry beyond their own congregation. In my Methodist tradition, we have a method for doing this we call apportioned or connectional giving. Other traditions have their expressions of this, too.

I've been in plenty of church meetings where we talked about our various ministries. Everyone shared enthusiasm over the ministries that cost little to no money: the cards the children made for the homebound members, the anthem the choir sang last Sunday, the prayer shawls that were knitted for the sick, and so forth. Sharing the love of God does not always have to cost money.

But when it came time to talk about ministries that did require funds, the mood changed dramatically. When it came to dollars and cents, it became more difficult for some to see the virtues of generosity and hospitality. But Paul encouraged the churches to be generous, for in so doing they furthered the gospel message. Hospitality necessitates generosity of spirit and giving.

Ultimately, the cause of Christ is served well when churches cooperate and do more to spread the good news together than any one church could do alone. For Jesus promised that we will do "even greater works" in his name (John 14:12).

Grant me a spirit of hospitality and generosity, Jesus, as you showed me yourself. Amen.

Luke 14:7-11

Table Manners

How can you apply Jesus' teachings to your everyday life?

When I was in middle school, my parents signed me up for Mrs. Gaddy's cotillion class. Over a series of Tuesday nights, boys and girls nervously gathered in the social hall of a community center in Raleigh as she taught us the basics of ballroom dance.

But Mrs. Gaddy also taught us manners and etiquette. It was a daunting task. Nevertheless, we learned the proper way to make introductions, to be gentlemen and ladies, to write invitations and thank-you cards, and to set a proper table. We practiced our table etiquette. No talking with your mouth full. No reaching across the table. Pass the salt and pepper as a pair. You get the idea.

So imagine this occasion in Luke 14:1-24, when Jesus went to the house of a prominent Pharisee as a guest and proceeded to lecture the host and the guests on who should be at the party and where they should sit! Jesus broke Mrs. Gaddy's rules for cotillion, and he certainly did not endear himself to his host or the other guests.

Nevertheless, Jesus taught them the true definition of humility and hospitality. Rather than inviting their rich friends for dinner, they ought to invite "the poor, crippled, lame, and blind" (Luke 14:13). And rather than taking the place of honor at the table, each person should "go and sit in the least important place" so that "you will be honored in the presence of all your fellow guests" when the host invites you to a higher seat (verse 10).

True humility (as opposed to false humility) is about a new way of being in community with one another in which the natural order of things is reversed. It's natural to assume that those who are socially high will be lifted up. We do it all the time: elevating celebrities, ceding power to the rich and powerful.

It's natural to assume that those who are socially low are low for a reason. Maybe they are lazy. Maybe they don't have the natural gifts or capacities to make their way in the world. That's the way the world sees them, but that's not how Jesus sees them. Jesus does not give special deference to rich people or the socially well-heeled. Neither does he look down on underprivileged people. He does not judge them on their bank accounts, their appearance, or their occupations.

Jesus is grieved and angry when he looks at how human beings have categorized and sorted themselves and one another into classes, hence, his stern teaching in today's text. True humility and hospitality are seen in how we treat one another. This is more than etiquette; this is ethics.

We would do well to remember that Jesus is our gracious host who has provided a great feast for all God's children. Jesus has shown us true humility and hospitality by including us in the first place. May we follow his example!

[1]*The United Methodist Hymnal*, 621.

Be present at our table, Lord, Be here and ev'ry where adored, These mercies bless, and grant that we may feast in Paradise with Thee. Amen.[1]

Joshua 1:1-9

Be Brave and Strong

How can you trust that God will be with you whatever you face?

Whenever we have a group in our local church that is going to go on a mission trip, I like to bring them before the congregation for a prayer of commissioning. It's a moment in which the people can pray for the safety and well-being of the missioners. At the same time, the missioners feel God's blessing on their work.

It's important to know God's hand is upon you when you make yourself available to God for mission and service. It's true for laity and clergy. Going out to answer God's call on your life is not something that comes at our own initiative. It comes from God.

We know this because we look back at examples like Joshua in the first chapter of the book that bears his name. This was after Moses' death. God charged Joshua with the task of leading the people into the Promised Land.

Joshua had been Moses' helper. He had shown his dedication to the Lord and the journey to the land that God was giving the Israelites. "I will be with you in the same way I was with Moses. I won't desert you or leave you," God promised (Joshua 1:5).

Of particular interest is the repetition of the phrase "brave and strong" in verses 6, 7, and 9. This was how Joshua should lead, by being brave and strong. God did not want Joshua to be afraid: "I am giving you every place where you set foot, exactly as I promised Moses" (verse 3). "Don't be alarmed or terrified,"

God assured Joshua, "because the LORD your God is with you wherever you go" (verse 9). He would have complete military success (verses 3-5), and God would never abandon him (verse 5).

No doubt, these were the kinds of concerns on Joshua's mind. He remembered the panicked voices of his fellow spies who reported that Canaan's people were too powerful and too strong and their cities too well fortified. So on this day, Joshua knew he needed to be commissioned by the Lord. There was no way he was going to go into this next stage of the journey without the Lord's full assurances.

As a commissioned leader, Joshua had certain responsibilities given to him by God. For one, he was "never [to] stop speaking about this Instruction scroll. Recite it day and night so you can carefully obey everything written in it" (Joshua 1:8). We believe this was a scroll of laws written down by Moses shortly before his death (referenced multiple times in Deuteronomy 28–31). Perhaps Moses believed that the people would eventually reject his teaching and leadership and reap bitter divine judgment.

The onus was also on the people, who needed to honor and respect Joshua's new authority. Only when Joshua and the people were adhering to God's guidance would they find success in the final stage to the Promised Land.

Grant me a brave and strong spirit, my Lord, as I follow your will; in Jesus' name. Amen.

John 14:25-27

The Hospitable Spirit of God

How can you know what Jesus would want you to do?

We do our best to follow Jesus' ways, to say the kinds of things he would say, to do the kinds of things he would do. But sometimes we are faced with circumstances and situations where the right way isn't always clear. There are a lot of matters that Jesus never spoke about directly. We must make certain inferences from what Jesus did say and try to apply his teaching to our complicated times. How can we do that? Should we even try? Can we trust ourselves to get it right? Surely, we need help.

That's where the Holy Spirit aids us. Jesus was clear to his disciples that the Father would send "The Companion, the Holy Spirit," to teach them everything and remind them of everything he told them (John 14:26). The tasks of the Spirit are complementary. It is said later on several occasions in the Gospels and Acts that the disciples remembered Jesus' sayings. Not only did they remember, however, they also were reminded. When they wondered what Jesus would do, the Spirit reminded them, and most of the time they followed suit.

What a relief that must have been. The disciples were scared, especially when Jesus talked about going to prepare a place for them (verse 3). They appreciated the gesture, but they didn't want Jesus to leave at all. Thomas said, "Lord, we don't know where you are going. How can we know the way?" (verse 5). And Philip said, "Lord, show us the Father; that will be enough for us" (verse 8), perhaps implying that he'd rather Jesus just show them the Father without leaving.

But it is because Jesus ascended to be with the Father, because he returned to glory, that the Holy Spirit was given to the early church (Acts 2). With the Holy Spirit, Jesus can be in all places at all times for his disciples.

As we look at the theme of hospitality in these readings, we are struck by the hospitality of the Holy Spirit. Just as we read yesterday that God would not abandon the Israelites, today we see God being faithful to send the Holy Spirit to be with us no matter what we face.

John often wrote of Jesus as the sent one, and so he was. Now Jesus' sentness will be seen in the Spirit as well. The same God who created heaven and earth has an affinity for dwelling in that creation, dwelling among the people in it. Through his Spirit, we are never left without Jesus' presence. The gracious host of the universe, the one John called "Logos" or "Word," is generous in hospitality toward us. As they say, a good host never abandons his or her guests.

When it comes time for us to make difficult decisions as Christians, we rely on the Holy Spirit. In prayer, fasting, supplication, Bible study, and in a host of other practices, we seek the Spirit's guidance. Sometimes we hear the Spirit rightly. Sometimes there is a communication breakdown on our end. But it is God's own hospitality that provides us with the presence of the third person of the Trinity. So we shall not be troubled or afraid (John 14:27)!

We thank you for the Holy Spirit, Triune God, and for your constant presence, reminding, and teaching. Amen.

Would Jesus have hung out with you?

Today, we are amazed to think that it has been 20 years since hijacked planes crashed into the World Trade Center towers, the Pentagon, and a field in Pennsylvania. That day, many cried out to God over the senseless tragedy and mourned the losses.

While questions still plague us, God has never abandoned us. The same Jesus who walked along the Galilean lakeside calling disciples and teaching people is the same Jesus who mourned with us on September 11, 2001. He is the same Jesus who will still come to set the world right. So even on this infamous day, we look at the stories of his life, we listen to his teachings, and we find comfort and calling.

Early on in the Gospel of Mark, Jesus began his earthly ministry by calling the tax collector Levi to join him. Not only that, but Jesus went to Levi's house, an unexpected destination for a rabbi who was expected to maintain certain codes of ritual purity. "Indeed, many of them had become his followers," Mark added (Mark 2:15).

This occasioned questions from those who watched: "Why is he eating with sinners and tax collectors" (verse 16). Jesus kept unpopular company. He intentionally spent time with people on the margins, people who were not part of respectable society. Jesus didn't just visit them, he ate with them.

While the distinction might be lost on us today, it was important to first-century Jews. A rabbi didn't just go around eating with tax collectors and sinners.

Jesus heard them asking one another why he was doing this. Perhaps they were asking with a loud whisper meant for him to overhear. Jesus' response was metaphorical, referencing the sick and doctors: "Healthy people don't need a doctor, but sick people do. I didn't come to call righteous people, but sinners" (verse 17).

On the topic of hospitality, note how (in the most common interpretations) Jesus shared the table at Levi's house. The Greek is actually not clear whose house it was, Jesus' or Levi's. But it was more likely Levi's since Jesus moved around in ministry and Jesus said the Son of Man had no place to lay his head (Matthew 8:20; Luke 9:58).

In either case, Jesus was the real host. The other guests were known only in relation to the fact that they shared a meal with him. Jesus demonstrated hospitality. He welcomed time spent with all people, but especially with those on the margins. He loves all people, even those who are judged by others. He is known for the company he keeps, for good or ill.

The way Mark tells this story, we are invited to find ourselves in it. Are we among the Pharisees who question Jesus' ability to judge character? Are we among the sinners and tax collectors at the table? If we are honest, we will admit that we are no better than any other sinners.

It is to us, then, that Jesus says, "Follow me" (Mark 2:14) and sits down to eat. We may be his "sick people" (verse 17); but if that is so, then we are the ones he has come to call.

Call me and share your table with me, Lord Jesus. For I am a sinner. Amen.

True Hospitality

How do you welcome someone into your heart?

Just like yesterday, today's text draws a striking contrast between Jesus' reaction to a sinner and the opinions of the Pharisees, who were watching him closely. This passage is the first of two about how a faithful woman responded to Jesus' presence. Luke describes this unnamed woman as "a woman from the city, a sinner" (Luke 7:37). He does not disclose the nature of her sin, but Jesus did not reject her. He set aside the social expectations that he should not be in the presence of one such as her.

This was a dinner hosted by "one of the Pharisees" (verse 36). Already, there is the implication that Jesus was in hostile territory. Nevertheless, the woman wet Jesus' feet with her tears. Luke does not tell us the reason for her crying. She went on to dry his feet with her hair, a sacrificial act that the Pharisee onlookers might have interpreted as overly sensual. Then the woman kissed Jesus' feet and poured her perfumed oil from an alabaster vase over them.

Jesus' host displayed behaviors that made him the antithesis to Jesus' hospitality. The host wondered, "If this man were a prophet, he would know what kind of woman is touching him. He would know that she is a sinner" (verse 39). He gave no thought to the possibility that Jesus did know she was a sinner but received her anyway.

In the rest of the passage, we learn that the host's name was Simon when Jesus confronted him, saying, "When I entered your home, you didn't give me water for my feet, but she wet my feet with tears and wiped them with her hair. You didn't greet me with a kiss, but she hasn't stopped kissing my feet since I came in. You didn't anoint my head with oil, but she has poured perfumed oil on my feet" (verses 44-46).

Luke contrasted Jesus' welcome and hospitality with Simon the Pharisee's. Now Jesus contrasted the woman's welcome and hospitality with Simon the Pharisee's, too! Her generosity of spirit even led to the forgiveness of her sins, another confounding thing for the other guests. It was their contention that only God can forgive sins. But they did not as yet understand Jesus' divinity. This did not stop Jesus, who turned to the woman and said, "Your faith has saved you. Go in peace" (verse 50).

Jesus demonstrated hospitality when he allowed the woman to worship him. The woman showed hospitality when she cared for Jesus. The host had welcomed Jesus into his home for a meal, so we might at first suppose that this was hospitality. But his was a superficial social and domestic action not rooted in true spiritual hospitality.

Just because we do not turn someone away from church, that does not mean we are being hospitable. Just because we even have someone over for a meal does not necessarily guarantee that we have lived up to Jesus' expectation of hospitality. For Jesus, true hospitality is in the heart, the welcome, and a generous spirit of welcome.

If Jesus forgives us of our sins, it is not because we have learned the proper etiquette and table manners. It is because we have made ourselves available to his presence and grace by worshiping him. May it be so!

Show me the true nature of hospitality, Lord Jesus, as I read the stories of your welcome and grace. Amen.

Offering Ourselves

What does God want from you?

Throughout history (and before recorded history) people have tried to approach God in some way. In places and times when they did not know the God of Israel, they worshiped another god or gods. Normally this included rituals such as chants and sacrifices. In some world religions, the focus has been on finding a spark of divinity within yourself or releasing yourself from your body. Someone somewhere at some time has tried just about any method of communing with a divine being or beings.

God's people have been given rituals for worship, too: religious seasons, religious texts, traditional practices. There is nothing wrong with these in and of themselves. In fact, God has proscribed many of them in the Hebrew Bible. Look through the Bible sometime and see how specific God was about things such as the size and construction of everything in the Tabernacle, for instance. The whole book of Psalms is a hymnal for God's people, full of songs and prayers that every faithful believer was to know.

But once in a while, a prophet came along to remind the people that the rituals were tools. The rituals can be good human practices that God uses to form and shape our spirits and lives. But the rituals were not themselves divine. The prayers were not magic words by which to summon God. The sacrifices were not tokens by which one automatically got an audience with the Lord.

The prophet Hosea told Ephraim and Judah that the Lord God desired "faithful love and not sacrifice, the knowledge of God instead of entirely burned offerings" (Hosea 6:6). These words might remind us of Psalm 51:16-17 in which the writer (traditionally David) says, "You don't want sacrifices. If I gave an entirely burned offering, you wouldn't be pleased. A broken spirit is my sacrifice, God. You won't despise a heart, God, that is broken and crushed."

The plain meaning is clear: A sacrificial and loving attitude of the heart is most important to God. If we have a lavish offering for God, that is fine, but only when our heart is in it.

Not many of us give God burned offerings but, rather, we offer God other gifts such as time, money, and talent. Some people have the capacity to give large gifts; but God wants their hearts to be in the right place first, to be humble and loving toward God. Again, we do not receive God's favor simply because we follow certain rituals. We do not summon God by means of our token sacrifices of any kind.

Why is this the case? Is it because God is too big to be moved by our meager rituals and offerings? Yes, that's part of it. God is God, and we are not. But what kind of people would we be for God if we were locked in a mere transactional relationship or quid pro quo? We wouldn't grow closer to God. We wouldn't learn lessons from our life with God.

Since God desires "faithful love and not sacrifice, the knowledge of God instead of entirely burned offerings" (Hosea 6:6), we can offer our best to God. And our best is ourselves because we were created in God's image!

[1] *Hymnal*, 399.

"Take my life, and let it be consecrated, Lord, to thee. . . . Take my will, and make it thine; it shall be no longer mine."[1] Amen.

1 Corinthians 12:4-11

The Spirit's Gifts

Is anyone more important to God than anyone else?

"There are different spiritual gifts but the same Spirit," wrote Paul to the church in Corinth (1 Corinthians 12:4). He elucidates different gifts that are given to different people and how each of them comes from the Spirit of God. Each of the gifts he lists has an important part to play in the larger Christian community.

Some people have a word of wisdom, he says. Others have a word of knowledge. Faith is given to one, gifts of healing to another. Miracles, prophecy, discernment, tongues and the interpretation of tongues, all are given to different people.

In our church, we held a spiritual gifts seminar in which people took inventory of their spiritual gifts. Some were surprised to learn what the inventory told them. But all were enlightened and encouraged. Furthermore, they let our nominations committee keep a copy of the inventories so we could see who has spiritual gifts matching the church's different needs in different areas of our ministry.

But for all the variety of gifts, they all have one thing in common, according to Paul: They are all given by the Spirit. Let's not breeze past that. Paul is quite explicit about this in how he refers each and every one of these gifts back to their source in the Spirit. In verses 8-9, every single gift is paired with "by the Spirit" or "according to the Spirit." Verse 10 has a rapid-fire list that leads to verse 11, where he says, "*All* these things are produced by the one and same Spirit" (italics added).

Just as Paul has given us examples of the diversity of gifts, he also tells us that the gifts are united in their source: the Spirit. They don't come from different spirits. We know, then, that spiritual gifts are arranged in the church to God's glory. The Spirit has given some one gift and some another. A church in which everyone has the same gift of the Spirit would be a strange church indeed!

Consider how Paul explains in the next verses how "Christ is just like the human body—a body is a unit and has many parts; and all the parts of the body are one body, even though there are many" (verse 12). The variety of gifts is like the variety of body parts, each one coming together to make up the church and the people of God. But there's one other point Paul drives home to his readers: These gifts come not from ourselves, but from the Spirit. We are not the source of the spiritual gifts.

This may seem obvious at first. But consider how we tend to see ourselves as self-made men and women. We like to think that we worked on ourselves until we earned our giftedness. But even our basic abilities are gifts from God.

In the spirit of Paul's letter to the Corinthians, our various gifts should not make us boast about ourselves. Rather, our spiritual gifts are a testimony to the greatness of God. The spiritual gifts enrich the community of the believers together, all to the glory of God. For we worship "the same God who produces all of them in everyone" (verse 6).

Thank you, gracious God, for my spiritual gifts and for the opportunity to worship you through them. Amen.

Agree With One Another

How can you bring people together in the name of Jesus?

In 1 Corinthians, Paul seems to be defending himself against detractors (or "auditors," as scholars euphemistically call them). Apparently, people came through the area criticizing Paul's authority as a Christian leader and teacher. The Corinthians were given to factions and cliques, some of them probably based on socioeconomic and status categories.

Our text for today is part of a larger section in which Paul hoped to regain his influence over the fledgling Christian community. They should not have been divided against one another, and he hoped to bring them together under one banner of Christ. "Instead, be restored with the same mind and the same purpose," he wrote (1 Corinthians 1:10).

We need to hear this today when Christian people are divided into so many rival factions. As I write this, we're dividing up even more. Jesus did not set us against one another, so our divisions must be coming from ourselves. Too often we categorize and dismiss people in ways that must break Jesus' heart. For in his long prayer to the Father, Jesus prayed that we would be one as he and the Father are one (John 17:21).

Don't get me wrong: I love the Christian tradition in which I came to know the Lord's love. I don't believe that Christian traditions or denominations are inherently bad at all. But when we turn the diversity of our traditions into differences between us, we fall into the practices Paul calls out in this letter.

Paul said that "Chloe's people" had informed him that the people were fighting with one another (verse 11). Some were saying that they belonged to Paul. Others claimed to follow Apollos. Still others followed Cephas. Then there were some who claimed to follow Christ, perhaps meaning that they were the true Christians. But Paul put these differences in stark relief: "Has Christ been divided? Was Paul crucified for you, or were you baptized in Paul's name? (1 Corinthians 1:13).

The people's unity or division was a witness to Christ and his legacy. If they were bitterly divided, who would want to follow Christ with them? Usually we find our lives already have enough division in them without having to add religious division. Rather, by being in unity we can provide a witness that is favorable to Christ's legacy on earth.

Paul wrote a similar message on unity to the church in Philippi. "Complete my joy," he said, "by thinking the same way, having the same love, being united, and agreeing with each other" (Philippians 2:2).

When we find that there are differences among the people of God, we should work together to find the similarities and agreements. Surely, we have more in common than what divides us. We ought to consider seriously whether a point of contention is worth dividing over. We should not underestimate the damage done to our witness when we divide into factions.

Our true unity comes as a gift from God who sent one Savior to us all. There are not different saviors for different groups of Christians. "Has Christ been divided?" (1 Corinthians 1:13). Someone may be quick to exclaim, "Of course not!" But let us consider whether our witness gives people the impression that he has.

May we all be united in your name, Lord Jesus. May the world see that we are one in you. Amen.

People Who Create Divisions

What should you do about a difficult person in the church?

We have a problem: Because the church is supposed to accept everyone the way Jesus did, we are wide open to "people who create divisions and problems" (Romans 16:17). Anyone and everyone can come to Jesus, and that's as it should be. People should feel welcome to bring their whole selves to Jesus, warts and all. Addictions, neuroses, spiritual war wounds, excess baggage—all of it can be brought before the cross of Jesus and left there.

The problem is that the church isn't always sophisticated and wise enough to shield itself from harm when people bring their troubles into the church and act them out. Few people (if any!) in a local church are equipped to defend the church against people who "are serving their own feelings" (verse 18). And of those few who are equipped, even fewer can afford to expend the kind of time and energy it takes to do such hard work. They don't come to church to do that. They come for spiritual sustenance as other people do.

So the care of troublesome people usually falls to the clergy. The social structure of the local church is often set up to funnel difficult people to the clergy anyway. Someone panhandling in the church parking lot? A church member blew up in a committee meeting with wild accusations? Go tell the preacher, they reason. She's better equipped to handle that sort of thing, they figure.

But is that the best course of action for the church? Is that wise stewardship of the "human resources" of the church? Most laity who work for businesses or corporations would not send the difficult person right to the CEO's office. There has to be a better way.

Some wise leaders in my denominational body set up a full-time conflict management expert for our churches to share. They saw that some churches were expending a lot of time, energy, and resources dealing with a few unhelpful individuals. In some cases, the organizational dysfunction had become toxic, affecting the church's witness and mission to make disciples.

It's taken a lot of hard work—a lot!— but it has made a difference, and no one has been turned away from Jesus' love in the process. Sometimes the most loving and Christian thing to do is to equip the people of God to resolve their differences in constructive and loving ways.

This is what Paul urged the Roman Christians to do: "to watch out for people who create divisions and problems against the teaching that you learned" (verse 17). By speaking the truth in love about their situation, they could deal with their dysfunctions and eventually heal the hurt. It may be difficult to read Paul telling the Christians to "keep away from them" (verse 17), but he would have them do so for the fulfillment of their purpose: to make disciples of Jesus Christ.

Order your church, Lord Jesus, with care and compassion to make more disciples who will take your name into all the earth. Amen.

Avoid Divisive People

What should you do about someone who is dividing the church?

Did you find Titus in your Bible? It's a small book near the end of the New Testament, but it's packed with practical and relevant advice for the church. It's one of the three pastoral epistles, along with 1 and 2 Timothy, traditionally attributed to Paul the apostle. In these letters, Paul was not writing to a whole church, but to an individual. Information on Titus the recipient is scarce. Paul wrote about journeying to Jerusalem accompanied by Titus, who was then dispatched to Corinth. Titus then went to the island of Crete before reuniting with Paul in Nicopolis.

From reading the letter to Titus, we gather that some Jewish Christians were being rebellious. "In fact, there are many who are rebellious people, loudmouths, and deceivers" (Titus 1:10). Some were deliberately leading the people astray. Paul expected Titus to go and correct them. "Remind them to submit to rulers and authorities," Paul said. "They should be obedient and ready to do every good thing. They shouldn't speak disrespectfully about anyone, but they should be peaceful, kind, and show complete courtesy toward everyone" (3:1-2).

Paul even conceded that he and others were once "foolish, disobedient, deceived, and slaves to our desires and various pleasures" (verse 3). But God saved them from such behaviors by mercy. "He did it through the washing of new birth and the renewing by the Holy Spirit, which God poured out upon us generously through Jesus Christ our savior" (verses 5-6).

Here is an astonishing thing: Jesus made such a difference in the believers that they changed their behavior. That ought not to astonish us. But it seems to happen so seldom today. Paul could identify in himself a before-Jesus Paul (or Saul) and an after-Jesus Paul. Can we see that in our own lives, too?

Certainly, Paul had a dramatic conversion experience to point to. But that is not the only way to be changed by becoming a Christ-follower. Paul's charge, Timothy, grew up in a Christian home under the influence of his mother, grandmother, and their church. Certainly, Paul would not say that Timothy was not a true apostle. The point is that there should be some identifiable difference in us by way of our faith in Jesus as Savior. There should be some fruit of our discipleship and service. When Jesus is in our hearts, there is a new creation.

The verses selected for this day describe behaviors of someone who has not experienced the renewing of their mind in Christ Jesus: "stupid controversies, genealogies, and fights about the Law" (verse 9). By genealogies, Paul probably meant fights over who had the best pedigree.

Not only should a Christian avoid such things, he or she should avoid people who are caught up in such things. This may be hard for some of us to hear. We suppose that just as Christ accepts everyone, the church should do the same. But the Bible counsels us to give a "first and second warning" to "a person who causes conflict." And if that person does not heed the warnings, "have nothing more to do" with them (verse 10).

It may be, then, that some reconciliation is God-sized. Only God, not our own human ingenuity, can deal with some barriers to authentic Christian community.

Come, Lord Jesus, and heal our divisions. Call all people to follow you and to be transformed by you. Amen.

Who is the greatest in the kingdom of heaven?

Jesus turned everything upside down! We thought we knew who the important people were. You could identify them by their clothes, their retinue, the way they held themselves, and by their age.

Everyone in Jesus' day understood that children were just unfinished people. They did not contribute to the economy. (If anything, they were a costly obligation.) They always needed something, and their noses were always running. They also did not know the great philosophers. What did they have that they could teach anyone? They were still learning themselves.

Jesus' disciples were students, too, though. In a world so influenced by Greek thought, there was a big power differential between a student and a teacher. The disciples revered Jesus as their teacher, and a teacher was not at all expected to learn from the students.

So the disciples asked Jesus one of their many questions in Matthew 18:1. It was a good question actually: "Who is the greatest in the kingdom of heaven?"

It should come as no surprise that the disciples asked this question. They had already made it a point to start figuring out who among them was going to sit at the Teacher's right and left hands. Order and hierarchy were important to them and to their surrounding culture. Part of their reason for asking, then, was probably to figure out where each of them stood in relation to the Teacher and what they needed to do to advance higher.

Like the great teacher he was, Jesus saw this as an educational opportunity, an ah-ha! moment, as teachers call it. So, instead of answering as they expected, Jesus "called a little child over to sit among the disciples" (verse 2). Notice that he did not point at the children as he did to the birds and the flowers as examples in the Sermon on the Mount. In this instance, he called a little child to come sit among the disciples. Already, Jesus was turning things upside down because a child would not normally be allowed to sit among the adults, much less the male adult students of a rabbi.

Imagine what it must have been like for that particular child! He or she was likely doing things children do, when all of a sudden Jesus called him or her to sit among the disciples.

Jesus then said, "I assure you that if you don't turn your lives around and become like this little child, you will definitely not enter the kingdom of heaven" (verse 3). Wait! He said unless they became like a child they would not even enter the kingdom of heaven? The child was suddenly no mere example of a particular childlike virtue. The child was already elevated to be a citizen of heaven!

This implied the disciples couldn't keep figuring out on their own how to wedge their way into heaven or how to vie for the best seat. No, none of that would work. They had to go through a transformation such that they became as a little child. (This might remind us of how Jesus spoke to Nicodemus about being born again/from above.)

The key to this transformation comes in humility. "Those who humble themselves like this little child will be the greatest in the kingdom of heaven," Jesus said (verse 4). This would require a whole reordering of the disciples' world, something only God could bring about.

Help me be humble, Lord Jesus, like the little child you brought before the disciples. Amen.

Jesus Brings People Together

How can divisions in your church be healed?

Today's reading is longer than most, but take time to read all of Galatians 2 if you can. You'll see a stark contrast between the first half of the chapter and the second (today's reading). If you stop at verse 10, you would think all was well. Paul enthusiastically proclaimed victory in the Jerusalem meeting. But then, at verse 11, things take a sharp turn.

It turns out that there had been a conflict at Antioch. Unity had been strained again, and it looks as if there was bad blood between Paul and Cephas (Peter). We're left to try to interpret the conflict, but Paul saw a parallel between his problem with Cephas and the situation with the Galatian Christians. We never get the conclusion to the Antioch problem in this letter.

Many scholars suspect that this means Paul lost the contest with Cephas. If he had convinced Cephas and the other Jewish Christians to accept his arguments, he would have said so. After all, that's what Paul did in verses 1-10 regarding the Jerusalem meeting. Paul was not one to downplay his successes.

The matter with the Galatians is clearer: The gospel called on Jewish Christians to form a new community in which there were no distinctions between Jewish Christians and Gentile Christians, where they ate together at table. Circumcision and food laws would take a backseat to Christ, who lived in them.

We see people put aside their differences and distinctions today to join in Christian community. Perhaps you have had the rare blessing of being in a church that is diverse in any number of ways. A few churches are racially diverse. Some churches are economically diverse. And all are made up of people with their own stories, experiences, opinions, and tastes.

The good news that Paul brings is that Christians can come together despite their differences. And there were numerous differences between the Jewish Christians and the Gentile Christians. The Christian community in Antioch was indeed a good example for Paul to point to. The Jerusalem meeting had formed a separate-but-equal Gentile mission but had not anticipated the differences among the people in Antioch.

By the grace of God in their midst, the Antioch Christians, Jew and Gentile alike, made a practice of eating together. But "certain people came from James" pressuring Peter to stop eating with Gentile believers (verse 12). But Paul says that he confronted Cephas about it and said, "If you, though you're a Jew, live like a Gentile and not like a Jew, how can you require the Gentiles to live like Jews?" (verse 14).

Today, we will do well to take a lesson from the church in Antioch and Galatia. They remind us that Christians can overcome differences among them by the presence of Jesus in their hearts. It is God's doing, not ours.

At the end of the day—and at the end of all the days—reconciliation and restoration of relationships are God's work. God graciously gives us an opportunity to participate through unity in Jesus Christ. Where the church dwells together in unity, Jesus is there.

Heal our brokenness and division, Lord Jesus. Break down the dividing walls among your people. Amen.

20

Micah 4:1-4

God Draws People In

What does God want for you and for all God's people?

God has a people. In the Hebrew Bible, the people are clearly defined: the descendants of Abraham. In the New Testament, the promises to Abraham are extended to Gentiles who proclaim Jesus as their Lord. The family of God grows, but all the while, God has a people.

In the ancient Near East, it was common for every city-state to have a deity to whom the citizens prayed. Battles between city-states were often cast by the scribes as battles between those respective city-state gods. So, it was said in the ancient writings that Yahweh was Israel's deity. Throughout the Hebrew Bible, the battles involving Israel were cast as battles between Yahweh and the enemy's god.

The same went for a city-state's prosperity. If a city-state enjoyed a time of plenty, the people of the other city-states would notice and associate that deity with power and benevolence. If the people suffered a time of famine, the neighboring nations would say derogatory things about that nation's god.

It became important for prophets like Micah to encourage God's people when times were tough by pointing to a future time when things would be better. For example, "in the days to come, the mountain of the LORD's house will be the highest of the mountains; it will be lifted above the hills; peoples will stream to it" (Micah 4:1). The "mountain of the LORD's house" will be higher than ("superior to") the mountains of the other nations. The peoples streaming to it will be from Israel and from the other nations. Therefore, "many nations will go and say: 'Come, let's go up to the mountain of the LORD, to the house of Jacob's God, so that he may teach us his ways and we may walk in God's paths!'" (verse 2).

What does this mean for us today? We can take assurance that God still has a people. And as Christians, we are part of God's people by the grace of Jesus Christ. We worship the same God who draws people to himself. As Jesus said, "When I am lifted up from the earth, I will draw everyone to me" (John 12:32). God draws people in. Jesus draws people in.

Now consider that God has invited us to be part of that drawing-in of people! Amazing! God has graciously given us a part to play in adding to God's people. Remember, they don't come to church to seek us. They come because they seek the Lord.

When we are an invitational and welcoming people, we participate in the promise Micah conveyed from God: that people will stream to the Lord's house (Micah 4:1). When we care for one another in God's family and in the church, we aren't just being good friends. It's even greater than that. We are participating in the blessings God gives to God's people, blessings that the prophets foretold!

Today's passage ends with a promise that we need to hear in our day and time: There will come a day when the nations will turn to Israel's God and dwell together in peace. "Nation will not take up sword against nation; they will no longer learn how to make war" (verse 3). The peace God offers us in our hearts will extend to become a peace between the nations. This is God's promise, and we are blessed to be God's people!

Draw all people to your temple, Holy God, through the love of Jesus Christ, in whose name I pray. Amen.

John 14:1-3

God's Hospitality

Where can you look for comfort when you are grieving?

Have you ever been away from home for a long time and yearned to return? Perhaps you pull into the driveway and see the lights on inside. Coming through the door, you are greeted by the embrace of loved ones. Your favorite dish is served at dinner, and you can't wait to sleep in your own bed again.

Or have you ever been the guest of an excellent host who has prepared his or her home for you? A lovely room is reserved for you. Everything you need is there. Your host has extended generous hospitality.

Jesus' words in John 14 were meant to convey God's hospitality. "My Father's house has room to spare," he told his worried disciples (verse 2). There would be plenty of room for them to join him someday, so they shouldn't be troubled (verse 1).

Keep in mind the context of these verses: It was after the Last Supper, and Judas had gone out to betray Jesus. As John tells it, Jesus then spoke at length to his disciples about how he would be leaving them. He was speaking of his crucifixion. He told them, "I go to prepare a place for you" (verse 3).

The disciples were scared. They asked, "How can we know the way?" (verse 5). But Jesus told them that he was the way (verse 6). In following him, they were following the way to the place where he was going.

This all must have seemed vague to the disciples at that time. They did not understand that Jesus would be resurrected and return to them in the near future. Looking back on it, writers like John could see what Jesus meant. They help us understand that God is our gracious host who has prepared a place for us in the eternal kingdom.

Today's passage is often read at Christian funerals because it is comforting for mourners to remember that God takes their loved ones to a place where the Father has "room to spare" (verse 2). In this way, the Holy Spirit reminds us that God has a place for us. We are not abandoned in this life or in the life to come. As Jesus said, "I will return and take you to be with me so that where I am you will be too" (verse 3).

But we do not need to confine this passage just to those times when we are in grief over a death. We can take encouragement from this promise when we feel alone or when we worry about the future. For example, a person who is faced with his or her own mortality can take great comfort in the promises of John 14. For as the Bible says, "All who call on the Lord's name will be saved" (Joel 2:32; Romans 10:13).

We do not always know what tomorrow may bring. We might face loss or grief and need these healing words. Our journey through life might feel like a long trip away from home. But God has prepared a place for us. The lights are on in our forever home where we will dwell with God. Everything has been prepared. Our room is ready. We will be welcomed. So let us not be troubled.

Grant me the comfort of your promises, Lord Jesus. Welcome me into your holy presence. Amen.

Appealing to Our Commonalities

How can you help people come to know the Lord God?

During one of his many journeys, Paul went to the major urban center of Athens. The city was the home of great arts, learning, and philosophy (Plato, Aristotle, and others). It was also religiously diverse. There were statues and temples to numerous gods and goddesses. There were the 12 major Olympian deities (Zeus and Hera, among others), and there were numerous cults.

Most Greeks of the time assumed that they should honor all the gods and goddesses they could. If someone neglected to worship a deity, that god or goddess might withhold blessings or even bring down calamity. So people went to great lengths to satiate all the deities they could.

But the ancient Athenians figured that one person couldn't possibly know all the gods and goddesses. What if one was left out simply because they were unknown? For this reason, there were altars constructed to honor unknown gods. Paul saw one of these on his way through Athens. He thought about it and realized that this was a way he could tell the Athenians about the Lord God he worshiped.

We read that Paul "was deeply distressed to find that the city was flooded with idols" (Acts 17:16). He talked to the Jewish and Gentile believers in the synagogue and addressed whoever would listen to him in the marketplace. This caught the attention of certain philosophers who took him to "the council on Mars Hill" (verse 19), where he was questioned about his teachings.

It was there that Paul stood up in the middle of their council and spoke the words we have in today's reading. He appealed to their religiosity because he saw that as a commonality among them. Then he mentioned the altar to the unknown god. He explained, "What you worship as unknown, I now proclaim to you. God, who made the world and everything in it, is Lord of heaven and earth" (verses 23-24).

See what Paul did there? He went into a foreign land among strangers who did not worship his God, and he appealed to their commonalities. Then he saw an opening in their practices into which he could speak to God's work in his life.

People today worship a lot of gods and idols, too. They may not always have proper names such as Poseidon or Ares. But they can have more subtle names such as power, wealth, and sex. Indeed, people build great temples and altars to these gods. Skyscrapers, malls, sports arenas, and other monuments might not seem religious at first. But think about them as being temples to the things we often worship. My seminary is part of a larger university at which there is a running joke that the basketball arena is the center of university religious life, not the on-campus chapel.

But as Paul explained, "God, who made the world and everything in it, is Lord of heaven and earth. He doesn't live in temples made with human hands" (verse 24). Paul's God—our God—is not like the ancient Athenian deities. Paul found a way to help the Athenians understand how his God is different by appealing to something the Athenians could understand and relate to. It is our task today to do the same.

Most high God, may the nations come to know you through the words of your servants of the past and today. Amen.

Philippians 2:9-11

God Highly Honored Him

What does Jesus' life have to teach you about power?

This week, our readings have been focused on how God has a people and a kingdom. Our passages have referenced the nations and the peoples of the world and how they are drawn to the Lord God. Today, we come to a portion of the famous Christ Hymn (Philippians 2:5-11) that Paul quoted in his letter to the Christians in Philippi.

In this hymn to Jesus, we hear, "Though he was in the form of God, he did not consider being equal with God something to exploit. But he emptied himself by taking the form of a slave and by becoming like human beings" (verses 6-7). Jesus ignored the privileges of his divinity and glory to be part of humanity.

But the hymn takes a dramatic turn in verse 9. It says that because Jesus "humbled himself by becoming obedient to the point of death, even death on a cross," then God highly honored him and exalted him (verses 8-9).

God gave Jesus "a name above all names" (verse 9). Just as Israel's God was compared to the gods of the neighboring city-states, so now Jesus' name is compared to all other names and found to be superior. This reminds us of Micah's statement that the nations will stream to God's holy mountain (Micah 4:1-4).

Jesus' name is so superior "that at the name of Jesus everyone in heaven, on earth, and under the earth might bow" (Philippians 2:10). Jesus is given the most superlative accolades. Not only will knees bow, but every knee will bow in heaven and on earth and under the earth.

Theologians refer to this as Jesus' glorification. They say that just as Jesus lowered himself to be among us, he was then glorified to be above us again. But in his glorification, he brought along his humanity—our humanity. Because he went to our level, we are swept up with him into glory.

But there's even more! The hymn ends with a promise "that at the name of Jesus . . . every tongue confess that Jesus Christ is Lord, to the glory of God the Father" (verses 10-11). Jesus is so glorified that everyone will confess him as Lord. Talk about a triumphant note!

To give someone a name is to give that person status and power. For Jesus, he now has the highest name, on par with the name of God. The idea that every knee shall bow and every tongue confess recalls Isaiah 45:23, where the prophet refers to the worship of God.

And for the people in Philippi who first read this letter, this meant that Jesus had a name higher than the Roman emperor! This was a consequential claim. The veneration of the Roman emperor had evolved into something of a cult itself by the time this letter was written. Rome had taken on otherworldly significance in the hearts and minds of many of its people.

But Jesus showed that true power is not found in the systems of domination familiar to the Romans and those under Roman rule like the Philippians. True exaltation and glorification come from humility and lowering oneself. Jesus is our prime example and helps us see this now, "to the glory of God the Father" (verse 11).

May we come to know your power and glory, Lord Jesus, by looking to your life of humility, to the glory of your name. Amen.

Holding on to Faith

How can you continue to have faith in God's promises?

Whenever we have trouble clinging to God's promises and plans, we can always look to those who came before us. In our church, we celebrate All Saints Sunday, for instance. Every year, we look back at those saints, those we have known personally and those we've known only by their names and reputations. We draw encouragement from them: how they lived their lives, how they put God first, and how they faced adversity. The living saints among us (the mothers and fathers of our faith in our local church, family, or neighborhood), they too provide us with examples to follow here and now.

In a way, we might look upon the Bible as a book of saints. From Genesis to Revelation, we find countless examples of people who persevered in faith. As the writer of Hebrews puts it, "The elders in the past were approved because they showed faith" (Hebrews 11:2). Indeed, Chapter 11 is a recitation of the saints and their faith.

The early Christians looked not just to the other followers of Jesus, but back to the patriarchs and matriarchs of the Hebrew Bible as well. Abel, Enoch, and Noah precede an extended reflection on Abraham and Sarah in verses 8-19. This is fitting since Abraham was the one who received God's covenant promise to bless him and his generations and to form a nation from them.

Hebrews tells us that "by faith Abraham obeyed," and by faith he lived in the land" (verses 8, 9). What did the author mean by "faith"? We just need to look at verse 1: "Faith is the reality of what we hope for, the proof of what we don't see." This implies a certain amount of human embrace and trust. But it is more than that. Faith is a gift from God, something that comes from beyond ourselves and our human capacity.

By faith, Abraham did three things: (1) he obeyed God's call to go to a strange place and inherit it (verses 8-10); (2) he and Sarah received the heir that God promised them (verses 11-12); and (3) he offered Isaac to God as he was instructed to do (verses 17-19).

This week, we focus especially on the first of these as we see that Abraham's obedience led to the people of God having a place to call their own. Indeed, Abraham's people "confessed that they were strangers and immigrants on earth," the Hebrews writer tells us (verse 13). And "people who say this kind of thing make it clear that they are looking for a homeland" (verse 14). So it was that God gave them a homeland. God has a people, and the people have a land.

We may feel lost and spiritually homeless sometimes, but we must remember the promises that were made to our ancestors in the faith and how they lived "by faith." God never abandoned them. Quite the contrary. God stayed faithful to them, even as they wandered away. "Therefore God isn't ashamed to be called their God—he has prepared a city for them" (verse 16).

Thank you, God, for giving us the examples of our fathers and mothers in the faith! May I hold fast to your promises as they did. Amen.

Dual Citizenship?

How can you put your allegiance to Jesus first in your life?

It's a safe bet that everyone reading this is a citizen of some country, even if we are not living there at the moment. And almost everyone has citizenship in a state, province, and/or county. Some are citizens of a town or a city. But it has not always been this way.

In the ancient Near East, citizenship in a city-state (often one under the control of Rome) was a privilege. People vied to get Roman citizenship, for example, because that came with great benefits. Others were named by their home family or household rather than by their civic citizenship.

So when Paul referred to himself and his fellow Christ-followers as citizens of heaven (Philippians 3:20), he was making a statement that was spiritual and political. In fact, in the Greek language, the word for "citizenship" refers to the commonwealth or state and also to the privileges and duties assigned to the people of that state.

Paul was saying, then, that being part of God's people through Jesus is like citizenship of a sort. It means being a citizen of heaven, that is, having one's identity and allegiance tied to one's faith rather than to one's birthplace or political entity. So Paul wrote, "Our citizenship is in heaven" (verse 20). By that, he meant we not only have a place in heaven, but we also have certain privileges and duties associated with that place.

The challenge of this idea is that we are led to think of the compatibilities and incompatibilities of our worldly citizenship and our heavenly citizenship. Where do they conform to one another? Where do they clash? Is it possible for us to have dual citizenship? What do we do if the state requires something of us that conflicts with what heaven requires of us?

This is not a new dilemma. Christians have had to live into their worldly citizenship while keeping their heavenly citizenship paramount. The great temptation is to set aside the primacy of our heavenly citizenship, to compromise on our sacred responsibilities to fit into our secular roles.

But Paul would not have us let this happen. He lifted up himself and the others who follow "this way" as examples. "You can use us as models," he wrote (verse 17). And how did Paul handle it? He spoke of our heavenly citizenship as something that already exists, but it is also to be brought to earth. He expected a hoped-for restoration of the world. "We look forward to a savior that comes from there—the Lord Jesus Christ. He will transform our humble bodies so that they are like his glorious body, by the power that also makes him able to subject all things to himself" (verses 20-21). This transformation is an echo of Jesus' humiliation/glorification Paul expressed in Philippians 2:5-11. It allows Christians to become like the Lord Jesus Christ.

Our present task is to remember our heavenly citizenship and our identity, our allegiance, and our obligations that come with that. We hope that we don't face an incompatibility between our heavenly citizenship and our civil citizenship. (Some Christians say if we do not see the incompatibility, we are not paying attention.) But if we do, we should be ready to make a faithful decision.

I thank you, heavenly Lord, for my place in your kingdom and all that comes with that. Keep me faithful to you. Amen.

Part of God's Household

What does it mean for you to be part of God's household?

Our readings this week have been about our dwelling, our nation, our citizenship, and other ways of describing this construction into which we have been granted admittance by the grace of God in Jesus Christ. Today, we read Ephesians 2:19-21 to find that we are the "whole building" and the "temple that is dedicated to the Lord" (verse 21). We are "God's household" (verse 20)!

Where once we (Gentile Christians) were strangers and aliens, now we belong to God's household. And as God's household, we "are built on the foundation of the apostles and prophets" (verse 20). We are part of the household that includes the saints recounted in Hebrews 11, and Christ Jesus himself is the cornerstone of this new household (verse 20).

Think about how this sounded to the people who first heard it, the church in Ephesus. Recall that the household was the basic building block of society in their time. A head of household had relatives, servants, and slaves living in the same residential complex. Foreigners or aliens might be living in the household, too.

So when the writer declared, "Now you are no longer strangers and aliens," he meant they were not guests in the household of Israel. They, and we, are members with the full rights and privileges that come with that. "You are fellow citizens with God's people, and you belong to God's household" (verse 19).

Then the writer used another metaphor: the temple. Jewish Christians undoubtedly knew the centrality of the Jerusalem Temple in their faith. Gentile Christians came to understand it in their own way. But now the two are part of the building up of a new temple (verses 21-22). To a Temple-oriented Jew, this was a bold statement, but the epistle means what it says. Jesus is the cornerstone of a new temple. Apostles and prophets are the foundation. And just as the Jerusalem Temple was the place where God held a presence in the world, so will the temple of believers be the place where Jesus is resident. As he said, "Where two or three are gathered in my name, I'm there with them" (Matthew 18:20).

The letter to the Ephesians emphasizes the unity of the Jewish Christians and the Gentile Christians. In Ephesians 2:14-15, the Law and the commandments are pictured as a wall that kept them apart, but now has been broken down. A new architectural style has been adopted, one in which Jesus Christ is the cornerstone.

In the new dwelling, God is present to the faithful through Jesus. All are invited to come and join God's people. The people dwell together in unity because of their bond in Jesus Christ. The new temple is a fulfillment of the promises made to Abraham and his descendants. It is strong and prosperous just as the prophets foretold.

And you are part of it through the power and grace of Jesus Christ! Thanks be to God!

Count me among your people, loving Lord. Number me among your faithful. Amen.

Genesis 28:1-5

Building the Family of the Lord

Why was it important that Jacob take a wife from within his family?

The history of the Hebrew faith started when God first spoke with Abram, but he only had one son who followed in worship of Yahweh. That son, Isaac, had two sons, but only Jacob was the keeper of the covenant. But Jacob was the father of the 12 tribes of Israel. It was his descendants who went to Egypt and were the people God rescued and brought to the Promised Land. While the story of faith began with Abram, the story of the Hebrew people began with Jacob.

So, it was important that Jacob find a wife who would not divert him from the faith. His brother, Esau, had married Canaanite women, much to his parents' distress. When Jacob sought a wife, his father told him to go to Paddan-aram, where his mother's kin lived. He needed to find a wife who would accept for herself his identity as a follower of God's covenant. What was crucial was not so much racial or ethnic purity, but a wife who would follow the Torah and obey God's laws.

The Hebrew Bible has complex and often contradictory teachings about intermarriage. Sometimes it was strictly forbidden and caused great difficulties, such as when King Solomon married foreign wives. But sometimes key Old Testament figures, such as Moses and Joseph, married women from different cultures. What seemed to make the difference between allowing intermarriage or forbidding it was the ability of a spouse's culture to influence the obedience of God's faithful followers and the willingness of their wives to embrace the faith of Yahweh. Moses' wife, Zipporah, for example, became a faithful witness to the demands of the Torah. But other times, the community of faith became accommodating to the culture around it and allowed other values to distort their faith. They conformed to the world, and that could not be allowed. If the Hebrew faith was to survive, it would have to be protected from the dominate cultures around it.

This is often true in the church today. There is a tension between the church being a force within the world and it being "of" the world, tempted to change key values and beliefs in order to fit in. God's Word from the beginning was radical and demanded a different way of living for believers. Imagine a faith that didn't allow work on the sabbath, especially in an agricultural society where harvest was the difference between life and death. Think on Jesus' radical call to love your neighbor in a land that was occupied by foreign forces. There has always been a strong temptation, even for believers, to conform to the values of society instead of the Word of God. This is why it was so important that the very beginning of the faith was forged with those who would commit themselves to the way of the Lord.

Lord, help me to balance being "in the world" with being "of the world." Amen.

28

Exodus 40:34-38

God's Glorious Presence

Where can we meet God?

The Hebrew people left Egypt and traveled through the wilderness for 40 years on their way to the Promised Land. God told Moses, their leader, to build a tabernacle, a portable earthly home where God would come to dwell with the people. God gave Moses specific instructions on how it was to be constructed, and the finest craftspeople worked to build it.

Many chapters in the Book of Exodus are devoted to step-by-step instructions and descriptions of the Tabernacle, and the people were careful to follow God's instructions exactly. Finally, it was finished. The people stood waiting. Would their work be pleasing to the Lord? Would God actually come to dwell with them?

God visibly came in a cloud and covered the meeting tent. God's presence was so powerful and profound that Moses couldn't enter the tent. The Hebrew people knew, in a concrete way, that God was with them. Their work was not in vain and God accepted their invitation to take up residence in their wilderness tent.

Of course, we believe that God is everywhere. There is no place in the cosmos where God is not. But there have always been places where the presence and power of God seem particularly strong. The ancient Celts called these places "thin places," where the barrier between the physical and spiritual seemed especially nebulous. By creating a tabernacle for the Lord, the Hebrews created their thin space where holiness was palpable.

This meeting tent, although quite different from today's modern churches, illustrates the most important elements of a church. An authentic church is a place where God is welcome and at home. At its best, worship creates a thin space there, and it becomes a place where one can feel the presence of the Lord.

The Hebrew people's meeting tent was portable, so when the cloud of God's presence lifted, they packed up and moved. In this way, God led them through the wilderness, signaling when it was time to rest in God's presence and when it was time to forge ahead.

Both elements—that of resting with the Lord and of moving forward in faith—are crucial for any spiritual community to grow in their relationship with God. The Tabernacle symbolizes not only God's abiding presence with the people, but God's continuing attendance with the people as they go out into the world to do divine work. While we often think of a church as a specific place, it is actually the place where God meets us.

This has been amply illustrated during the pandemic when church buildings were closed. God was not shut out. God continues to meet people in living rooms, in outdoor worship, or in acts of service. Our God is always ready to meet us where we make a home for God.

Lord, may my life be full of thin spaces where I can especially feel your presence. Amen.

Matthew 18:15-18

Reconciliation Within the Body of Christ

How can we protect the integrity of the church family from sin in a spirit of love?

Whenever I've read about deathbed regrets, people have rarely mentioned their achievements or careers. They almost always speak about relationships: what they could have done better and how they could have protected them. In the end, our relationships with God and with others are the most important things in our lives. They can often take a lot of effort to maintain, but relationships are precious and worth the work of reconciliation.

Relationships within the church are no exception. This passage is part of Jesus' instructions to the new community of believers who were the kernel of the church. These instructions are based on longtime Jewish traditions about conflict within a faith community. They are not instructions for minor grievances among members, but for serious infractions against the community of believers. They offer a blueprint for intervention with forgiveness and reconciliation as a goal. Thus, it's hard work, done not in a spirit of revenge or compensation, but of coming together again in love.

The first step, when there are problems, is a one-on-one intervention. This is to protect the accused from humiliation. If the problem can be solved by a quiet talk among caring friends, so much the better. If that does not work, then Jesus suggested that the offended person bring several more from the congregation to talk to the offender. That way, there are witnesses, and also a chance for both sides of the story to be told.

If that doesn't work, then the issue is to be brought before the entire church for discussion. If the offender is still unrepentant, then he or she is to be treated "like a Gentile or tax collector" (Matthew 18:17). This doesn't mean that they are to be ignored or shunned, however. Remember that Jesus regularly ate with Gentiles and tax collectors. It means that they are to be considered unbelievers, but with the ever-present offer of grace and reconciliation to rejoin the fold if they repent.

Today, many people just drift away from a church community without much intervention. However, Jesus asks us to expend a lot of effort on those who are going astray. In following these instructions, the entire church community could become involved in calling back an errant member. Relationships with our brothers and sisters in Christ are to be treasured and are worth the effort to preserve them.

Verse 18 tells us that whatever is fastened on earth is also fastened in heaven, meaning that when a church asks a member to leave, they are doing it in the name and authority of God, and so it is a deeply serious event. The hope is always that an errant member can be welcomed back in joy and once again become a member of the body of Christ.

Lord, may my church always strive to deal with sin with a spirit of love and reconciliation. Amen.

Jesus Dwells in Our Agreement

Can we expect God to fulfill every one of our prayers if we pray properly?

Some years back, I was in a Sunday school class, and one of the members, a roofer, had a bad fall. He was near death. The leader of the class quoted Matthew 18:19 and led us in prayer for his healing. When he died, the leader accused us of doubting God and said that was the reason our prayers weren't answered. The class split apart in grief and confusion, upset by our apparent lack of faith and confused about the Scripture that had seemed to promise his healing.

I have since learned that the leader took this verse completely out of context and, as a result, it was profoundly damaging to the faith of many people in that class. Taken out of context, this verse can completely pervert the character of God and our relationship with God.

God is not a magic "Santa Claus in the Sky" who will grant any wish that two or more people voice together. Think of the power that would take away from God if that were true. God would only then exist to fulfill our wishes, without a will of God's own. To believe that we have the power and ability to dictate what God should do is not only disrespectful to God, but terrifying in that we, as mere human beings, often don't know what is best.

We need to read this verse in its context to understand what it is saying. It's within a discourse about church discipline and resolving disagreements within the church. The verses around this one speak of working toward reconciliation with forgiveness, mercy, and compassion as key elements of that process.

Christ's promise is that he is among the decision-makers when there is a sincere effort to reconcile an errant member. And if people come to an agreement within that process of Christ-centered decision-making, be it between the original offender and others or between the members of the church, then God will uphold the decision that is made. Because Jesus Christ has been a member of the deciding body, then the decision is bound in heaven as it is on earth.

Taken in this way, the verse and the ones that surround it point us to the importance of seriously considering our actions as a church body regarding those whose actions are harming the congregation. It's a matter that concerns Christ enough that he considers himself one of the decision-makers, and it's a decision that has ramifications all the way to heaven.

The story of the lost sheep, which Jesus recounted just before his instructions on church discipline, show just how important every believer is to him. As a congregation of Christ-followers, we should value every believer with as much love, care, and compassion as Jesus does.

Lord, guide us in the decisions we make for the health and well-being of your people, the church. Amen.

Acts 14:21-27

Perseverance

How did Paul respond to rejection of the Word?

Elisabeth Howard was born in 1926 and grew up in Moorestown, New Jersey, the same town in which I was born. She attended Wheaton College and studied classical Greek because she felt her calling was to translate the Bible into obscure languages. She traveled to Ecuador to evangelize the native Quichua tribe and there married Jim Elliott, who was also working with them. Three years later, her husband was speared to death with four of his missionary friends by the members of a neighboring tribe. Their daughter was only ten months old.

One would think that Elisabeth would take her baby and go home. But Elisabeth asked members of the Quichua tribe to teach her the Huao language so that she could communicate with the tribe that had killed her husband. Two years later, she and her daughter went to live with the Huaorani tribe to teach them of the love of Jesus Christ. She stayed in Ecuador until 1963, translating the Bible and spreading the love of Jesus Christ.

When the apostle Paul went to Lystra, he was attacked, stoned, and left for dead (Acts 14:19); but this passage says that soon after he recovered, he returned there. He went to minister to those who had tried to kill him and "strengthened the disciples and urged them to remain strong in the faith" (verse 22). Their persecution only helped in the growth of the faith. Paul told them that they had to pass through many troubles, but he didn't allow even attempted murder to stop him in his quest to make new disciples for Jesus Christ.

Boldness for Jesus Christ can be dangerous. Thankfully, it's not often life-threatening, but Jesus spoke a counter-cultural message that challenges the ways of life of many who hear it. Love your neighbor, and even your enemy! Blessed are the poor! Turn the other cheek! It's not the way people naturally live, and living by these words can disturb the status quo.

But like the churches begun by Paul and Elisabeth Elliot, God blesses those who live by the words of Christ. Their churches grew and strengthened, and they were able to "open the door of faith" to others who could then see the light of Christ (verse 27).

I think that it wasn't just the words that Paul and Elisabeth Elliot said when they returned to teach the Word of God; it was their presence in the midst of adversity. The story of Jesus was so important that they could not leave others without it. Their return with a message of love and forgiveness, even after being persecuted, must have done much to turn the hearts of those who heard them. Their boldness for Jesus Christ brought others to salvation.

May our churches remain bold in speaking of the radical love of Jesus Christ for all!

Lord, give me the courage to be persistent for you, even in the face of suffering and difficulty. Amen.

Strengthening the Faith Community

How can a church maintain a strong and healthy congregation?

Other than the church, can you name another institution that has lasted over 2,000 years? I think the reason the church has lasted for so long is that it isn't a human institution, but an institution of God. But it still needs care and dedication to stay strong, healthy, and growing.

The Letter to the Hebrews is actually less a letter than a sermon to a congregation that was waning in faith, attendance, and commitment. The members were suffering persecution and were becoming disillusioned because Christ had not yet returned. They were beginning to wonder if what they believed was true and if the suffering they were withstanding for the faith was worth it all.

This entire passage (just one long sentence in the Greek) speaks of three things the congregation had to do to strengthen their faith. The first thing was to draw near to God.

Before Jesus Christ, the Temple was built with a sacred inner room, the Holy of Holies, where the ark of the covenant was kept. That was thought to be the dwelling place of God. Only the high priest could enter the Holy of Holies once a year. But because of the sacrifice of Christ, we all have been made pure and clean enough to be able to enter this most holy place. We all are welcome to make a home in God's most intimate and personal space because we are part of the family of God, called to be in the very presence of the Lord.

The second thing this letter told this struggling congregation to do was to hold onto their hope. They could be certain that every promise made by Christ is true. This was especially important for those who were becoming impatient for Christ's return and beginning to doubt.

The third instruction for this church was to motivate one another in love and good deeds. Actually, the Greek word used for "motivate" is closer to "pester" or "provoke"! This apathetic church needed to be prodded into action! Often, we think about what we do wrong, but this reminds us that not doing right when God gives us the opportunity can be just as bad.

These instructions are relevant for the church of today. Drawing near to God means we are active in worship, prayer, and study, always nurturing our relationship with the Lord. Holding onto hope means we keep confidence in our faith. And motivating one another in love and good deeds means we are built to do God's work on earth. When we become deaf to God's call to strengthen and serve others, we lose our purpose as people of God.

The writer of Hebrews questioned how a church could accept the gift of salvation and do anything less. May we value Christ's love for us with the same passion in our worship, prayer, and service.

Lord, help my church draw near to you, keep our confidence in you, and always serve you. Amen.

Acts 2:37-47

Changing the World

What did the early church do that made it so strong and fast-growing?

Margaret Mead, an American anthropologist, said, "Never doubt that a small group of thoughtful, committed, citizens can change the world. Indeed, it is the only thing that ever has."

Perhaps no other small, committed group has ever made a bigger impact than the people who formed the first Christian churches on Pentecost, after Peter told a crowd about Jesus Christ's offer of salvation. About 3,000 people joined the few hundred others who had been followers of Jesus Christ. They dedicated themselves to Christ's teaching and to the community they built together. Today there are 2.3 billion practicing Christians who, with God's continuing guidance and help, have impacted the world in incredible ways.

When the people heard Peter, they cried out, "What should we do?" (Acts 2:37). How could they join in and claim this gift of salvation? Peter told them to repent and be baptized. They were to turn from their old ways of life and commit themselves to living by the Spirit and the Word. This was a new idea for most of these people. Religion in the ancient Greco-Roman world was generally not a life-changing thing, but just a practice of occasional cultic acts to convince specific deities to favor them. Their religious beliefs did not affect how they behaved in their day-to-day life.

But to follow Christ meant that they would live their lives with a totally different focus. This was not just a religion but a radical new lifestyle. They joined the community of believers and devoted themselves to one another's care. This early church is probably the only instance in Scripture where people actually followed the Jubilee, the practice described in Leviticus 25 that realigned wealth and possessions among God's followers.

Sharing of possessions in the early church gets a lot of attention today because it's so radical, but even more important are the other ways they grew in faith together. They "devoted themselves to the apostles' teaching" and focused on learning the true word and how it would impact their lives (Acts 2:42).

They became a community, breaking bread together despite social conventions and barriers between different economic classes. In a society in which status and the company you kept were everything, treating the poor or even slaves as equals was unheard of. They prayed together, making their relationship with God their priority. God was not just an occasional duty for them. Instead, they were bonded to the Lord, empowered by the Spirit to become an authentic image of Christ in the community.

How can we apply this to our churches today? Life in the Spirit is not another thing to add to our to-do list, but is a way to be. It is a commitment to the community and to God that directs and focuses our entire lives.

Lord, may your Spirit permeate our congregations and strengthen our bonds with one another and with you. Amen.

4

Ecclesiastes 4:9-12

The Power of a Community

Why is it important to be part of a community of faith?

My hobby is fiber arts. I love to knit, and I enjoy weaving on my loom. Through the years, I've learned a lot about fiber, especially different kinds of yarns.

Most yarns are plyed. This means there are at least two strands of yarn that are twisted together. Unplyed yarns, which are only one strand, are fragile and therefore can't be used for many things. But by twisting two or more strands of yarns together, they become much stronger and therefore much more useful.

This short passage in Ecclesiastes applies this same concept to people. Two people working as a team can accomplish much more together than alone. When one tires or is injured, the other can pick up the slack. One person's knowledge, skills, and abilities can augment those of the other person.

Some commentators have suggested that this passage might be referring to marriage. Two people can keep each other warm at night, and the third cord in verse 12 might refer to a child. But whatever relationship it is suggesting, the point remains that people need one another for efficiency, security, comfort, and safety.

In the verses just before this passage, the writer talks of the pointlessness of living alone without any companions and working hard for basically nothing. The value in life lies in relationships, which enrich each person's daily life. While the overall tone of the Book of Ecclesiastes is depressing and discouraging, this passage is a rare bright point in the author's discourse. Relationships and companions are what make life fruitful and secure.

The writer was originally speaking on a broader scale, but it's certainly not difficult to apply this concept of companionship and support to the church. We can each go our own way in our faith, but if something causes us to stumble or fall spiritually, it's crucial to have another to offer his or her hand to raise us back up again.

Studying the Word together can help keep the flame of faith burning and help us maintain a strong commitment to God. People working together to obey God's call in the world can accomplish much more than just one lone person. God gave us one another for a reason, which is to encourage and strengthen one another when times get hard and to work together with our varied skills and abilities to do God's work in the world.

I can't warp my loom with one-ply yarn. The yarn needs to be in tension to get a good weave, and one-ply will pull apart under that stress. We live in a world full of tension and stress, so as a church, we need to depend on one another to keep our faith, our commitment, and our works in the Lord strong. By joining together, we can weave a strong and beautiful community of faith.

Lord, help our church to rely on your power and the power of the community you create for us. Amen.

5

Encouraging One Another in Faith

What can others teach us about our own faith?

The church in Rome was going through difficult times when Paul wrote the great Letter to the Romans. In the late 40s AD, Emperor Claudius expelled the Jewish community from Rome. There was a strong anti-Jewish sentiment in Rome, so most people, including Gentile Christians, were happy to see them go.

But in AD 54, Nero, the new emperor, allowed the Jewish people to return to Rome. Some of these people had since converted to Christianity, and the Christian church in Rome was struggling with the Jewish people returning. They took up their property and positions again, but many also joined the churches. So how could a church meld Gentile and Jewish backgrounds into one working entity? How did the history of the Jewish people relate to the story of Christianity? Paul's letter, written in the late 50s AD., attempted to answer these questions for the Gentile Christians.

Paul did not start the church in Rome. Unlike nearly every other epistle, he was not writing to people who were familiar with him. Therefore, his tone was not nearly as forceful or didactic as some of his other letters, such as his letters to the Corinthians. In this passage, located in the beginning of the book, he lamented that he was not able to come visit them. He wanted to spend time with them to encourage their faith and teach them, but also hoped that they could return the favor and encourage him as well.

Consider Paul's situation. Although a pillar of the new church, he was a Jew, a former Pharisee, writing to Gentiles who were struggling with their relationship with Jews. He had much to teach this new congregation, but he made sure they knew he was open to instruction and encouragement by them. It was to be a mutually supportive relationship, and he respected the faith they had already demonstrated.

It has often seemed to me that God enriches each of us with different strengths in our faith. I enjoy scholarship and like to teach others about the meaning, history, and background of the Word. Other people's faith is more heavily steeped in service or in deep prayer or a pure and simple trust in the care of the Lord. Spending time with people God has enriched in other ways is deeply encouraging to my faith as well.

When Paul visited these fledgling churches, he could not only instruct them, but could also experience the different ways the Spirit was working in their lives. I think that this would be an important thing for him to point out to a church that was struggling with division. Each person in the church, be they Jew or Gentile, could encourage and strengthen the faith of another if they were open to working together and learning from one another.

Lord, may my heart be open to the faith of others so that I may learn from and be encouraged by them. Amen.

Why is it important that every Christian be a vibrant member of the church?

Last night, my husband, my daughter, her friend, and I all worked to make a wonderful dinner together, largely from vegetables we had grown in the garden. As we ate, we talked about the work that went into this meal, even over the course of several months.

My husband helped me to build the raised beds to grow the vegetables. I started the plants from seed, planted them, and watered them every day. Yesterday, my daughter and I picked them. She and her friend made the salad while I put together the casserole. My husband cleaned up the dishes afterward. But all together, we created something nourishing and delicious! Of course, God made the vegetables grow so that we had such wonderful food, so God's part in it was so much greater than any of ours. But when we all combined our efforts, we made something wonderful.

Paul wrote this passage to a church that was struggling with incorporating Jews and Gentiles. Paul reminded them their strength came not from their similarity, but from their diversity of gifts and abilities. If they all contributed their God-given talents, together they could build something that would nourish their faith and the faith of others. Paul was asking them to respond in grace with their talents and abilities that came from God in the service of God.

It was and still is the way that grace should be evident in the daily lives of Christians. Using the gifts that God has given us, we are to nourish the world with our service.

Paul's list of talents and abilities in this passage name just a few of the blessings God gives us. Paul has more complete lists in other passages, most notably 1 Corinthians 12 and Ephesians 4. Except for prophecy, most of the gifts listed here are "ordinary" gifts that we generally don't think take extraordinary talents. I think his point is that everyone can contribute. There is a job for everyone, and we should not think too highly of any ability we might have that would elevate us above anyone else. The greatest chef in the world can't cook if no one grows the food.

Every Christian is intimately connected to Christ. Paul even said that each one of us is part of Christ's body. But that also means that each Christian is just as connected to every other Christian.

We think of being members of a church, believing that this means individuals who have joined up with others in something like a club. But Paul speaks of members as being part of a body, where everyone is crucial to the health of the whole. A body that is missing a hand, an eye, or an organ is certainly less effective and may even die. Each one of us is necessary to the well-being and strength of the body of Christ, his church.

Lord, guide me to my place within your church so I can be a valued part of your body. Amen.

Galatians 6:1-5

Carrying Burdens Together

What are our responsibilities to others in our congregation?

Many years ago, I had a disagreement with someone else in my church. Honestly, I don't even remember what it was about, but I do remember that I was certain I was right and he was wrong, and I was quite vocal about it. A good friend of mine took me aside and gently chastised me. She told me that my complaining was not good for the people of the church and that I needed to pray about my behavior. I was surprised and taken aback, but I realized she was right. After prayer, I apologized and let the matter go.

Our culture is based on individuality and responsibility for just oneself. But my friend demonstrated true Christian behavior as reflected in this passage and took it upon herself to call out my bad conduct. Paul told the Galatians that as a community of faith, they were responsible for the well-being of one another. It was their responsibility to guide one another back into obedience and to help heal rifts or transgressions when they saw them happening. Each person in the church has a duty to take care of his or her congregation's spiritual life.

But couldn't that cause trouble? I'm sure that many people would say that it's nobody's business what they do or don't do, and they don't need anyone telling them how to conduct their lives, spiritual or otherwise! Paul understood the problems in his counsel, too. His next sentence was a warning. The only way to counsel another was in a spirit of gentleness and humility, knowing that everyone can benefit from some correction now and again.

Giving counsel was not to be an act of superiority but of taking up the burden of another, just as Christ took up our burdens of sin. By being concerned with the welfare of others and the welfare of the church, a member who counsels others in love and in prayer is acting as a servant, not as one who lords over others and tells them what to do. What this means is that members of a church should respond with love and compassion to one another, guiding one another in growth in the faith and helping one another through their struggles.

Verses 4 and 5 might seem at first to contradict what the previous verses said. However, they are talking about ultimate responsibility. Each one of us must one day stand before the Lord in judgment for our own works and our own misdeeds. While we are to help our faith communities grow and flourish by routing out sin and offenses, in the end, each one of must personally answer to the Lord for our own actions. No one then can take our place.

But in the meantime, if we are to live as Christ, then we have the responsibility not only to offer counsel, but to take counsel from others so that everyone in the community of God can grow and mature into true disciples of Jesus Christ.

Lord, give me and those in my church the proper discernment to counsel one another in our spiritual growth. Amen.

Caring for the Sick

How does the church care for those who are suffering?

As I write this, the world is dealing with the effects of an international pandemic. Our lives have been dramatically interrupted, including how we live as the church. It's been a challenge for all of us to practice how to remain a community of God while we have been restricted in our ability to be with one another physically. It's also been a lesson in how to deal with illness, especially an illness that we didn't know much about and didn't know how to cure. What are our responsibilities as a faith community to one another in these circumstances?

Much has been written about this particular passage because of the emphatic way James writes about the power of prayer to heal. The passage has often been interpreted to say that if people are righteous enough, they can pray away illness. However, we know all of us eventually will die and that God has the ultimate authority over all events. Even righteous people can't dictate what God should do.

Verse 16 deserves some thought: "For this reason, confess your sins to each other and pray for each other so that you may be healed. The prayer of the righteous person is powerful in what it can do." While prayer may be answered in physical healing, the passage is actually more concerned with spiritual healing, which might well be the way that God would choose to answer a prayer for an ill person. But even beyond that debate, the point of this passage is how the community of the church responds to those who are suffering. What are our responsibilities to those who are weak, suffering, and alone?

Notice that the sick person called together the community of the church for solace, and the church responded. This recent pandemic demanded quarantines and social distancing, but there are other diseases or conditions that are nearly as isolating. Mental illness is especially segregating. Those with dementia are often forgotten in nursing homes. But in this passage, the sick were not forgotten. They were still members of the church community and were comforted with their care, prayers, and spiritual nourishment.

As members of a Christian community, this passage is reminding us that we have a responsibility to our members who need care, be it physical, emotional, or spiritual. As we surround them in love, God becomes active in our involvement, offering whatever healing is appropriate for the situation. The strength of God's care is reflected in the power of the community of faith and all are able to draw upon it.

It's easiest to focus on those who are strong physically, mentally, and spiritually and can contribute the most to the life of the church. But by caring for those who are weak and suffering, we as a church have the chance to heal along with those who need healing and to see God at work, in whatever way God chooses to act in each situation.

Lord, help us as a church to care for those who are suffering, and open our eyes to your many ways of healing. Amen.

9

1 Corinthians 12:12-13

All Baptized
Into One Body

How does discord in the church harm Christ's work in the world?

In the time that Paul was writing this letter to the Corinthians, the Roman Empire was dealing with rebels who were protesting Roman rule. While the rebels were never a serious threat, they were nevertheless still prevalent and a nuisance. Even one of the 12 disciples, Simon the Zealot, was a rebel.

One of the common ways that the Roman governors argued against these rebels was to compare the Empire to a human body. If one of the body's organs were to rebel against the rest of the body, the body would suffer. In the same way, these rebels were causing the smooth working of society to suffer. So when Paul used the analogy of the human body as a description of the church, his readers were familiar with the image he presented.

The church as a body was different, however, in that joining the body was the choice of each member. Paul wrote that each of them became part this body at his or her baptism. In fact, it is thought that part of verse 13 came from the blessing that each person received during baptism.

So by being baptized, each individual joined into the body of Christ, becoming part of the whole. They were unified in Christ. Their individual differences were no longer of any importance. This was a radical thought in Corinth. Corinth was a melting pot of many different cultures and many who were newly rich. They were concerned about advancing up through the social structure, so they were careful to be seen with the "right people."

For Paul to tell them there was no difference between a slave or a free person, for example, would have been shocking. Most likely, his words would have been rejected by those who were more concerned with being in the upper crust of society than being a vital part of the new Christian church.

If having the spirit of Jesus Christ within them made them into one being, infighting and contention among members was as damaging as if a body part decided to rebel against the body. It's significant that Paul only used this analogy of the body with congregations who were having difficulties within themselves. Because they were familiar with the analogy teaching that dissent damaged the whole, he was subtly reminding them that their discord was damaging the very body of Christ.

The health of any church depends on the unity among members. Perhaps that is why, sadly, many churches today are made up of people who are similar, usually the same ethnicity or social status. If we are to be the body of Christ, then every person who "drinks of the Spirit" is an important member of the family of God and should be a welcome member of any congregation.

Lord, may our church reflect a healthy body of Christ. Amen.

10

Honoring Every Part of the Body

Who are the unsung members of your church's congregation?

A few years ago, my daughter had a serious infection, and the doctors discussed removing her spleen. Personally, I've gone for years without thinking about my spleen. But when I learned about its role in fighting off infections, I was grateful I had one, and even more grateful when they didn't have to remove my daughter's and she fully recovered.

When Paul wrote about the church being a body, he was trying to make two points. The first, discussed in yesterday's reading, is that everyone in the church is interconnected and discord hurts everyone. The second is that each person in the church, although with different talents and abilities, is important. Even members who work behind the scenes or are not well-known are indispensable. They could be thought of as the spleens of the church!

Eyes, ears, hands, feet—all of these body parts get a lot of attention and are considered essential. Likewise, those in the church who were visible and accomplished high-profile things probably seemed to be more valuable. Remember that Corinth was a "new money" city full of people concerned with upward mobility. Those who were wealthy or who had powerful friends may have thought of themselves as the most important elements of the church. After all, they could pull the right strings, pay the bills, and make things happen. Like often happens today, the church could be a good place to demonstrate one's influence.

But notice that Paul didn't write this passage to the powerful members telling them they weren't as important as they thought, although there is a call to humility within the passage. Paul wrote this passage to those who were behind the scenes. They could be thought of as the spleens, toes, gall bladders, and the like who didn't see their own importance.

But the spleen wards off damaging infections, the toes help us keep our balance, and gall bladders filter out waste from our blood. All these things allow the body to maintain itself in health. Those who pray for the church to keep it in harmony, who help the church to balance its priorities or mitigate dissention in the congregation, are allowing the church to maintain its health, too. No one is unimportant to the body of Christ.

It takes all kinds of parts to make up a body. The church also needs people of different talents and abilities to be healthy. Paul reminded the Corinthians that God put their church together, not arranging it so that the "lesser" members serve the "greater" ones, but so that all might work together for a healthy and vital congregation. By valuing every member and bringing them into the life of the church, congregations benefit from a diversity of talents, gifts, and abilities.

Lord, thank you for every member of our congregation. Help me to appreciate what each person brings to our community. Amen.

11

Proverbs 18:15-17

Discernment and Wisdom

Why is it important to be able to change our minds?

When the internet was first developed, I read that it would be a new dawn of knowledge and information. For the first time, people would have the wisdom of the world at their fingertips. Any question we had could be answered by a simple query. What no one seemed to have considered was just how much misinformation would be on the internet as well!

People are using the internet to spread their own unsubstantiated opinions and untruths. We have to verify everything we find on the internet. Just believing the first thing we see is almost a guarantee that we'll be dealing with misinformation.

But these verses in Proverbs tell us that this problem is only one of scale, not born of a new technology. People have been spreading misinformation since the beginning of time. In order to be wise, we have to be discerning, double-checking information and determining where that information came from.

Verse 16, which talks about gifts, seems a little out of place in a discussion about discernment and wisdom until we realize the importance of gifts in the ancient society when Proverbs was written. Then the economy was largely barter-based, so many times in trading, transactions we would consider strictly economic took on the character of gifts. One person's indebtedness to another because of gifts could lead to corruption or to bribery. The writer here was warning against obligations that could be used to influence others in dubious ways.

Being discerning means having an open mind. Verse 17 tells of a trial where a witness presented a strong case that sounded reasonable. But after listening to a different witness, the writer realized that he didn't have all the information. By listening to a second witness, another opinion, or conflicting information and considering it carefully, a person comes closer to gaining true knowledge.

Quickly rejecting another point of view because it does not match our own doesn't lead to wisdom. Verse 2 in the same chapter says, "Fools find no pleasure in understanding, but only in expressing their opinion." It's crucial to listen to and understand both sides of a question before arriving at an answer.

Our current readings deal with interactions within the church community, so these proverbs remind us not to jump to conclusions about others. It can be a difficult thing to reexamine long-held beliefs or question biases we may have about others or other viewpoints, but this passage tells us that a sincere desire to know all the facts is a key to wisdom. Being aware of our biases is the first step. Being open to change our minds is true wisdom.

Lord, teach me to be open to new knowledge and understanding and to be discerning of what I hear. Amen.

Test the Spirits

How do you know if your spiritual beliefs are being improperly influenced?

On my bookshelf is a book called *Twisted Scriptures: Breaking Free From Churches That Abuse* by Mary Alice Chrnaloger. In it, she writes about organizations that misuse Scripture to control others. Instead of offering the freedom and liberty that comes from following Christ, they prey on self-doubt and equate spiritual discipline with obedience to church leaders. What a tragic situation! Instead of the strength and confidence that comes with living within Christ, their followers are shackled in insecurity and miss out on the joy of Christian living.

The early church faced problems like this, too. Some people claimed to be teachers of Jesus Christ, but they had twisted Christ's messages and were spreading false and even dangerous teachings. Chief among them were the Gnostics. They taught that Jesus wasn't a human being and had not come "in the flesh," because a divine being would reject sinful flesh. John opposed that teaching adamantly, saying that this was the "spirit of the antichrist" (1 John 4:3). Jesus was fully divine but fully human as well, and John taught that accepting both sides of his nature is crucial to knowing Christ.

So how do we know if we're being influenced to follow false beliefs? John was clear that there were those who taught as though they were Christian who were not. He wrote that God was within the hearts of true believers, and that they could be guided by God's Spirit to know the truth. God is greater than any force in the world, and the spirit of truth will guide believers through prayer, careful study, and discernment.

An effective way to discern truth is by observing how others respect Christ's teachings. Those who are open to the way of Jesus will respect it when they hear it. Those who are not will not listen.

There are basic tenets of Jesus Christ: to love God, to love and care for our neighbor, and to value our relationship with God above all others. Anyone who rejects those beliefs cannot be trusted, even if that person claims to be a believer. Anyone who actually knows God will resonate with those beliefs, not only in words, but in actions.

The key of John's teaching is that God guides the maturity and growth of believers, and God is the one who is worthy of trusting with our spiritual lives. It's easy to be swayed by the crowd and to be led into false beliefs. But because God is within every believer, there is a spirit that can be tested and trusted. Often the way of Christ clashes with culture, but by devoting ourselves to the Lord, we can rest assured that God will not lead us astray.

Lord, protect my faith and teach me to recognize your guidance as I mature spiritually. Amen.

Growing Toward Maturity

Why should we always challenge ourselves to grow in faith?

Every skill takes practice. Aristotle said that the way to become a harpist was to play the harp. In the same way, he said that the way to become brave or virtuous was to act bravely or virtuously and eventually it would become second nature.

Apparently, the readers of Hebrews were not doing that because they were having difficulties practicing the teachings of Christianity. They were not progressing and becoming strong Christians. Clearly, the writer of Hebrews was frustrated with them. By this time, they should have been teaching others and bringing them into the faith, but it wasn't happening. This passage was a challenge to them to "step it up" and prove to him that they could shake off their spiritual laziness and mature further in the faith.

Note that the writer was not saying they were incapable of understanding, but they had not been taking their spiritual growth seriously. Sometimes this passage is used to say that new believers cannot understand difficult concepts of faith, but no spiritual wisdom should ever be withheld from a believer. The writer didn't believe they were unable to understand Christ's teachings because in the verses that follow, he went on to explain the same difficult tenets he just accused them of being too immature to understand. Jesus said he never kept any teachings secret. He said, "I've spoken openly to the world. . . . I've said nothing in private" (John 18:20).

The point that the writer was trying to make is that spiritual maturity takes work, and that to grow in discernment, we must take our faith seriously. It takes wisdom and maturity to discern between good and evil. It's not always cut and dried. Following God's will takes not only the desire to do it, but the wisdom to know what God desires.

Wisdom comes from practice. Even mature Christians can sometimes fail in their discernment, but they try again, using prayer and study to guide themselves. This helps them grow, but if they don't practice the faith, they don't become strong and secure in their discernment. This is what the writer meant when he wrote that the readers weren't ready for solid food. Because they hadn't worked toward spiritual maturity, they were still "babies" in the faith (Hebrews 5:13) when it came to following the will of God.

The way to develop any ability is to challenge yourself to grow in knowledge and skill by practicing it. Far from being a warning not to get in too deep, this passage is a challenge to push ourselves further and grow in faith. It is only through the spiritual maturity that comes from prayer, study, and practice that followers can learn to discern and follow the will of God, leading to a life of fulfillment in Christ.

Lord, help me to grow in spiritual maturity so that my service to you may please you. Amen.

14

John 7:19-24

Understanding God's Commandments

How could misunderstanding God's laws thwart God's work in the world?

There is a famous story about New Delhi during the time of British occupation. Cobras were infesting the streets, and in order to control the deadly snakes, British officers offered bounties for dead cobras. At first, it worked. The cobra population dropped. But then, more and more people brought in dead snakes while the wild population remained stable. It was discovered that people had begun breeding cobras in order to collect the bounties. And when the bounty system was abolished, the captive cobras were released, increasing the snake population even more!

The Law was a good idea with a good goal, but it soon became perverted by people using it to their own advantage. In this passage, Jesus came up against people who had perverted the law of Moses. Moses' law forbade work on the sabbath. This was so that people would have time to consider their relationship with God and rest in God's care. It was a good law with a good purpose. But the religious authorities had perverted it, and instead of a day of rest and communion with God, sabbath had become a minefield of legalities about what was considered work that would break the commandment.

John 5 recounts Jesus healing a man on the sabbath. God calls us to care for others in need. Jesus responded to the man in the way God would have desired, but the religious authorities condemned him because he had violated their tangle of sabbath rules. They were actually using the sabbath commandment to keep people from serving God, the very opposite of its intent.

Jesus pointed out their hypocrisy. A Jewish baby boy had to be circumcised eight days after birth, even if that eighth day was the sabbath. Why was that allowed while healing was forbidden? Why would there ever be a time when it would be sinful to serve another? They needed to look at the law differently, responding to its intent as a call to serve God. They needed to take a step back from their laws and regulations, asking themselves what were God's true desires and how could they be served.

God's desires are for us to love and serve God and to love our fellow human beings as ourselves. What misunderstandings of religious law today stand in the way of us fulfilling those desires? Are there any people we exclude from the love of God because we don't feel they qualify? Jesus told us not to judge according to appearances, but with the desires of God in mind.

Faithful living challenges us to see the world through God's eyes, rejecting anything that stands in the way of serving God, holding the love of the Lord and of neighbor paramount to anything else.

Lord, open my eyes to your desires and help me to fulfill them. Amen.

15

Hosea 14:8-9

Wisdom and Discernment

How can we learn to discern the path of righteousness?

The Book of Hosea is a passionate account of the relationship between God and Israel cast as a marriage between an unfaithful wife and a suffering husband. Although the book is problematic because of the violent reaction of the husband to the wife's promiscuity, it clearly articulates God's pain when God's beloved people turned away. The story ends with their reconciliation and recommitment to one another.

This passage is the last two verses of the entire book. Much of Chapter 14 describes God as a beautiful tree that sheltered Israel, freely loving and caring for her after their reconciliation. God's shade protected her from the hot desert sun, and the tree offered her fruit to eat. Despite her unfaithfulness, God once again welcomed her with abundant love and care.

The final verse of Hosea is a summary of the lesson of the entire book. It sounds like a verse out of Proverbs, seeped in the wisdom tradition. It tells us that those who walk in the ways of the Lord, obeying God's commandments and being faithful to God, are upright and righteous. Those who are not will stumble.

This makes it sound like doing the right thing is the easy thing, but we all know that it is not. Doing the right thing means having that difficult conversation; passing on temptation, even when we doubt we'll get caught; and having to do something that may hurt someone we care about. Even the righteous often stumble on the path of obedience to God.

Sometimes it's not even clear what the right thing is!

That's where discernment comes in. The beginning of verse 9 tells us that the wise and discerning are able to know what is right. One key step of discernment is recognizing there is an issue or problem that needs to be addressed. Doing the wrong thing can sneak up on us when we do something just this once or just a little bit. Before we know it, we're on the wrong path.

Discernment takes maturity and the ability to see things for what they are, not what we want them to be. Discernment asks that we are honest with ourselves and aware of how our actions or beliefs are affecting us and others around us. That's often more than we're able to do, so that's why we're instructed to pray. The beautiful hymn "What a Friend We Have in Jesus" states, "O, what peace we often forfeit, O, what needless pain we bear, All because we do not carry everything to God in prayer."

Conversations with God can be our most trusted means of discernment if we're open to often uncomfortable or unwelcome truths that God tells us. But it doesn't end on just knowing the right path. To be righteous means we commit ourselves to following the path God has shown us. Those who do can find life in the shelter of the Lord.

Lord, teach me the difficult task of discernment. May I always listen to your guidance. Amen.

Proverbs 18:1-2

Seeking Connection With Others

Why is it important to listen to others, even if you disagree with them?

During the time of COVID-19, most of us had to adjust to much less social activity. Scientists and medical professionals were concerned about mental health during this time because human beings are social creatures. Being within a community helps people test their beliefs against those of others and take other's needs and desires into consideration. Isolation can cause people to focus only on their own beliefs and desires, sometimes becoming so set in their thoughts that it is difficult to reason with them.

Ironically, instead of helping with this problem, social networking may actually exacerbate it. Online communities can become "echo chambers" where people interact only with others who have the same thoughts and beliefs. Conspiracy theories thrive on social media because people feed one anothers' fears. People can begin to isolate themselves only with others who think as they do, fostering extreme beliefs that no one can reason away.

This seems to be a modern problem, but remarkably, these two verses in Proverbs speak to this same situation! Those who isolate themselves, either from others or just from disparate viewpoints, can become indulgent and selfish, refusing to consider the thoughts or needs of others. True wisdom, the verses tell us, comes from being in community and being open to listening to everyone. In order to be wise, we must have the capacity to understand others, even if we don't agree. The ability to empathize with others, even in controversial situations, can work toward achieving sound solutions to contentious problems. "Know it alls" actually don't know much at all except their untested opinions.

Perhaps you've never thought of being opinionated as being selfish, but if your opinions keep you from considering the situations of other people, that is exactly what these verses say about those who refuse to consider another person's point of view.

Verse 2 says, "Fools find no pleasure in understanding," which implies that wise people enjoy understanding the viewpoints of others. Understanding why others believe what they believe can't help but foster harmony because that understanding is a search for common ground. It's respecting others enough to hear their stories.

And isn't that what Jesus did? Jesus ate and drank with those others rejected. He listened to their stories and sought to understand their hearts. It didn't mean that he had to agree with them, but it meant he cared enough to find a place of connection with them. Seeking that place of connection is not only wise, but it's the way of Christ.

Lord, open my mind to hear the thoughts of others so that we may find a place of connection. Amen.

Who do you say that Jesus is?

My images of Jesus have changed throughout my life. From the pictures I saw of him in Sunday school as a child, I believed he was a nice, long-haired man in a long robe who apparently liked children and sheep.

When I was in college, the musical *Godspell* was popular. In it, Jesus was a magical clown who was thoughtful and kind to everyone. Then *Jesus Christ Superstar* portrayed him as misunderstood and trapped in the thankless role of a revolutionary before his time.

Popular culture continues to give Jesus different personas. Even the four Gospels portray him in different lights. Wars have been fought over the question of his humanity versus his divinity. "Who is Jesus?" is a question that is still controversial over 2,000 years after he walked the earth.

When Jesus asked his disciples who people said he was, they named prophets from the past who spoke with power about God and who had confronted authority. Like the images of Christ throughout my life, they had gotten parts of who Jesus was but far from the entire picture.

When Jesus asked Peter who he thought he was, however, Peter responded, "You are the Christ, the Son of the Living God" (Matthew 16:16). Peter confessed that Jesus was the fulfillment of the deep hope of Israel for its Messiah and was intimately connected to the Creator God as his human yet divine Son. He knew this not because anyone told him so, but because God had revealed it to him. His understanding was a gift from God. It wasn't because Peter was especially spiritually insightful, but because God had bent down to him to bless him with this realization.

This is how many of us come to faith. We may think we know who Jesus is, calling him a great teacher, a social reformer, a healer, a revolutionary, or a humanitarian. All have a kernel of truth, but to limit him to any or all of these descriptions is to try to conform him to human understanding. We finally learn who Jesus is not by watching or studying him, but by knowing him. We come to know Jesus by entering into a relationship with him—a relationship that is initiated by invitation only. That's when we come to understand his true self.

This relationship is the basis of the church. Christ told Peter that he would build his church on him, the "rock" (verse 18). Peter, filled with the Holy Spirit, later spoke to crowds at Pentecost, bringing thousands to the light of Jesus Christ. But although Peter's role in the church was unique, his understanding of Jesus Christ is available to all who accept the invitation to relationship and come to realize who Jesus is.

Lord, thank you for your invitation for a relationship with you. May I know you and, in so doing, know who you are. Amen.

18

Proverbs 4:20-23

Guarding God's Words

How do God's words impact your life?

One of the challenges of reading Scripture is that we're not reading it in its original language. The Proverbs, of course, were originally written in ancient Hebrew. Because we can often be influenced by the words chosen by a translator, it's a good idea to study Scripture with more than one translation. That way, you can see if there is a word in the passage that could be translated in a different way, giving you a new insight on its meaning.

This passage is a good example. If you are using the New International Version or the New Revised Standard Version, verses 21 and 23 contain the word "heart." However, if you read the Common English Bible, the Hebrew word used there, *lebab*, is translated as "mind." In our culture, when we say *heart* in such a context, we are usually speaking of our emotions. Using *mind* means that we are relying on reason. And so when the author wrote to protect or guard one's *lebab*, we could understand this to mean to keep our emotions under control or to make sure we are careful about what we believe.

So which is correct? Actually, the Hebrew word *lebab* has connotations of heart and mind. While the word *lebab* referred to the organ of the heart, it also referred to the origin of someone's will and thought. Most important for our discussion, the *lebab* held a person's true inclinations toward God on a conscious and subconscious level. A good or strong *lebab* would hold the basis of a person's wisdom or righteousness. It would be where one's reasoned and spontaneous actions would originate.

So if a person were to keep God's words in their *lebab*, that would mean God's teaching would be at the center of their being. God's Word would be the source of their actions and the basis of their thoughts. To guard one's *lebab* would mean to nurture right thinking, right inclinations, and a right moral code.

This passage instructs us to hear and to see. People can often become so focused on unimportant things that they lose awareness of what is happening around them. God may be whispering to them but they don't hear God's call. Jesus often ended his parables by saying, "He who has ears to hear, let them listen." If we do, we will recognize the words of the Lord.

Therefore, we are to keep ourselves alert and aware for the movement and impact of God in our lives. When we recognize God's work, we are to open our hearts and minds to bring God into the center of our being, allowing God to be the driving force in our lives, consciously and in our spontaneous actions. Because the words of God are our very life-force, we are admonished to protect their place in our *lebab*, our heart and mind, and let God's words be our guiding force in all that we do.

Lord, open my eyes and ears so that my heart and mind will belong to you. Amen.

Joy Within Repentance

Why would someone celebrate when they became aware of sin in their life?

In 587 BC, Jerusalem was conquered by the Babylonians, and the elite of Judah were taken to Babylon. The Babylonians found that if they assimilated the educated and ruling classes of those they had conquered into Babylonian culture, the conflicting cultures stopped fighting them. In this way, the Babylonians had already destroyed the Amorite, Kassite, and Chaldean cultures. The Book of Daniel is largely about the resistance of some of these Hebrew exiles to assimilation and their faithfulness to the Lord.

However, 50 years later, Babylon was conquered and the victorious king, Cyrus, allowed the Hebrew people to return home to Jerusalem. The books of Ezra and Nehemiah tell of their return home and their rebuilding not only of the Temple and city walls, but of their community of faith in the Lord.

The people requested that Ezra read God's law to them. They gathered together to hear the Torah, standing for hours. When Ezra was finished, they were heartsick. It was clear their way of life was not following the laws and was not pleasing to the Lord.

However, Ezra told the people not to mourn. He designated the day as holy and told them to celebrate! This was to be a new beginning, a new start for their relationship with the Lord. They were to celebrate the Festival of the Tabernacles in joy and gratitude for God's deliverance.

That's because while God's Word lays bare our sin, it also offers us the solution. Repentance is followed by commitment to a new way of life. God's law outlines the remedy. It also makes us aware of how our lifestyle affects others. Ezra commanded the people to bring food to those who didn't have food for a feast. If God offered mercy and compassion to those who had sinned, then it was only right for those with plenty to offer their surplus to others in the same spirit. The true test of faith is not what we know, but what we do when we know.

And that's where there is peace. Faced with the tragedy of their sin, Ezra told them not to be sad because "the joy of the LORD is your strength" (Nehemiah 8:10). They had the assurance of God's character, works, and care for them. They were not in an untenable situation alone, but were rescued by God, ushered into a new way of life, and promised God's everlasting *hesed*, or steadfast love. By remembering the power of the Lord, the guidance of God's teaching, and the call to help others, the people were able to turn their lives around to a new vision of the future.

Although our failures are often difficult to deal with, we can rest in the assurance that God is there to lead us out of the messes we've often created for ourselves. Awareness is the first step toward joy in a new life of righteousness!

Lord, thank you for your grace, which allows a new life for every sinner. Amen.

New Cloth and Wineskins

How do Jesus' teachings integrate the old and the new?

I was a teacher during the time education was transitioning from chalkboards to Smartboards. Personally, I loved the Smartboards and the new things we could do with the technology. But a Smartboard didn't make a good teacher. We still needed to use particular teaching techniques and methods in order to be effective, whether we were using new technology or not. Smartboards didn't abolish teaching theory; it expanded the possibilities.

This passage in Matthew addresses how Jesus' new way of living challenged old thoughts. Often, this passage is interpreted to mean that Judaism, the old way, had to be discarded in favor of the new thoughts and practices of Christianity. But closer reading reveals that's not the intent. Matthew 9:17 speaks of preserving the old and the new. Each has value.

Looking at the passage in context shows that it is set within incidents where Jesus was questioned by the Pharisees, who represented conventional religious thought. Even the disciples asked Jesus about fasting, which was an old practice, and its place in worship. Jesus didn't tell them to discard old ways. Instead, he told them he was there to show them new ways of living into the old.

Matthew's Gospel emphasizes how Jesus had fulfilled the prophecies of old. In Matthew 5:17, Jesus said, "Don't even begin to think that I have come to do away with the Law and the Prophets. I haven't come to do away with them but to fulfill them." He didn't come to discard the old, but to show how the new realized those prophecies in ways that shattered old ideas. They were fresh ways of seeing things that didn't fit into the confined thinking of conventional religion.

Trying to force Jesus' new vision of the kingdom of God into rigid and unyielding religious practices would be like putting new wine into old wineskins. An old wineskin would burst under the pressure. Jesus was telling his disciples that nothing could contain what he had come to do! Following Jesus means to think big and outside the box. Jesus showed humanity new ways of responding to the call of the Lord.

Following the Law meant an eye for an eye, but under the broader, more expansive way of Christ, he told his followers to turn the other cheek. The Law said to love your neighbor, but Jesus taught to love your enemies as well.

The love of God that Jesus taught was not limited by only what had to be done. Jesus went beyond the Law to a new way of completeness, of showing God's love to all.

Lord, help me to live beyond the Law and into your vision of the kingdom of heaven, here on earth. Amen.

Romans 12:9-13

Love—Genuine!

How do Christians live out God's love within their community?

This morning, I opened my email to a note from my pastor. He said that through his years in ministry, he felt one of the surest signs of spiritual health in a church is how the congregation responds to the needs of its elderly members, people he calls "wisdom people." As people who have been active in the church become less mobile or unable to drive, a church that has a true spirit of Christianity will make sure they are cared for. These important elderly members will have food in their homes and rides to doctors and other services because their family in Christ will respond to their needs in love.

This is exactly what Paul was writing about in this passage. In the Greek, verse 9 begins with the simple command, "Love—Genuine!" After that, he listed ways in which the family of Christ shows genuine love to one another and to others outside the family. The grammatical structure of this passage suggests that it was translated from Hebrew and was taken from an early Christian Jewish community. That would suggest it offers a glimpse into the structures of early Christian society.

The passage starts with a broad command. We should hate that which is evil and hurts others. This is the basis for all the other commands. Love is unhypocritical and will always consider the good of others, so if we let love guide our actions and completely reject evil, then the details of proper behavior probably don't have to be spelled out. Love like this results in a natural behavior born of living within the Holy Spirit.

Loving one another means respecting one another. Verse 10 talks of loving one another as members of one's family and honoring one another. An ancient translation of this text says, "Show the way to one another in respect." This love comes from an enthusiastic embracing of the Holy Spirit. How could a love like that be anything but genuine?

If a church demonstrated a love like that to its members, its "wisdom people" would be cared for, like my pastor wrote. So would its children, its struggling parents, and its needy. All of the members would be eagerly and enthusiastically looking for ways to demonstrate God's love to one another. Our everyday lives would demonstrate the love and grace of Jesus Christ.

Chapter 12 ends with this strong challenge: "Don't be defeated by evil, but defeat evil with good" (verse 21). Evil is strong, but the love of Christ is even stronger. Just as Jesus defeated death on the cross by demonstrating the greatest love of all, our call as Christians is to harness the power of goodness and grace and to demonstrate it to our own community and then out into the world. They will know we are Christians by our love!

Lord, may my life be a reflection of your grace and love! Amen.

22

Haggai 1:13-15

Joining Together in Obedience

Why would you obey a God you barely know?

Imagine if your parents had been uprooted from their homeland and exiled to a foreign country where you were born. Your entire life, you heard about the land of your roots, although you'd never been there yourself. Sixty years later, a generation removed from the exile, you were allowed to return. What would you do?

When the elite of the Hebrew people were taken from their home in Judah and brought to Babylon, many elected to stay when they were able to return. The Babylonians worked hard to assimilate those they had conquered, and for a large percentage of the Hebrew people, it worked. They changed religions, customs, and language and became Babylonians. But for those who wanted to go back to Judah and reclaim their heritage, it was difficult to return.

When they got back to Judah, they found that over the course of 60 years, their land and possessions had been claimed by others. Their Temple, the center of their faith, had been destroyed. For many, they didn't even know much about their religion anymore. Although they were in their homeland, a place they had longed to return, when they actually got there, it was strange and even foreign to them. How could they rebuild a home there, and rebuild themselves into a community of faith?

This is the setting of the Book of Haggai. We don't know much about the prophet himself, but amazingly, the dates of each event in Haggai are preserved to the day. We know that the events in this passage happened on October 17, 520 BC. The people were frustrated and struggling to survive in a ruined city. But through Haggai, the people heard that the Lord was with them, and God "moved the spirit" of the leaders and of the rest of the people (Haggai 1:14). Together they joined one another to work on rebuilding the Temple, even in the face of their own devastation.

God sent the people a prophet to deliver a divine message. We don't know how God moved or stirred the spirit of the people, but they responded. Verse 12 says that they "feared" the Lord and so obeyed.

Obeying someone in fear sounds terrible, but the meaning of "fear" here is closer to awe and wonder. The people weren't cowering before God, obeying because they were terrified of what God would do to them if they didn't. Instead, as they learned about the Lord, they became amazed that such a glorious and powerful God would choose to be with them, and they responded in gratitude to please God. Instead of a fear that diminished them, God's power empowered them. God's inspiration caught up the entire community and they worked together to rebuild their Temple.

Lord, stir the spirit of my faith community so that we will work together to do your will. Amen.

Building Up the Community

How do spiritual gifts strengthen the church?

We've probably all been in meetings where individuals, perhaps with an inflated opinion of themselves, dominate the conversation with their "wisdom and knowledge" that actually isn't useful or is irrelevant. It can be difficult to get things done in these circumstances. It soon becomes clear that their goal isn't to solve the problems that the meeting was called to address but to show everyone else just how important and knowledgeable they are.

Perhaps this is how Paul felt about glossolalia, or speaking in tongues. It was considered one of the greatest spiritual gifts from God, so those who had the ability to speak in tongues often felt as though they were more important to the church than others. In Corinth, glossolalia rivals often talked over one another in tongues and weren't polite enough to try to listen to one another. It wasn't a time of spiritual strengthening, but a free-for-all for status. It wasn't helping the community grow in faith at all.

Paul instead praised prophecy. Prophecy, in this case, was not an ability to tell the future, but to speak words everyone could understand and that were inspired by the Holy Spirit. First Corinthians 14:25 suggests that prophecy could include holy insight into problems of someone's heart. Paul believed that all Christians could have the gift of prophecy, so unlike glossolalia, it didn't bestow greater status on an individual. In fact, the authority in prophecy was because of the Spirit inspiring the words, not in who was speaking. Maybe we have had the experience of hearing someone speak stunning words of truth that changed our insight. The speaker may have said that the words "just came from the Lord" and were unplanned. This is the kind of prophecy, a revelation of God's truth, that Paul was speaking about.

However, it didn't have the same authority as Scripture, and it needed to be considered, weighed, and judged. But unlike glossolalia, it could work to build up the church. And isn't that the goal of everything we should be doing for our faith community? Paul told the Corinthians that their goals were not personal elevation, but to strengthen and encourage one another. All that is good for the community of God has love as its motivation.

Glossolalia isn't usually a major issue in churches today, but sometimes pride is, and this is what Paul was speaking against. Paul certainly wasn't upset with people having spiritual gifts, but he was concerned with how they were being used. When we think about gifts or abilities we offer to the church, we should assess them on their value to the faith community, not on how they make us appear to others.

Lord, thank you for the spiritual gifts you have given my congregation. Guide us to use them to strengthen our community. Amen.

24

Revelation 3:1-6, 14-20

Spiritual Malaise

What are some of the dangers that can destroy a community of faith?

The Book of Revelation was written about the year AD 95, after churches were established throughout the ancient Near East. It begins with seven short letters to churches, explaining their strengths and weaknesses, written in the voice of Christ. Today's passage is to two of the churches, Sardis and Laodicea, both of which were losing their faith and were in danger of failing.

Sardis was a city in decline. Like the city, the church was dying. The letter referred to their main product, cloth, by telling them their clothing was stained. They had reverted to worshiping idols and false images of Jesus; and their once white robes, symbols of their faith, were ruined. Jesus reminded them that he would return and see their heresies. He called on them to repent and turn back to him so that they could walk with the few faithful saints there who remained.

Laodicea, in contrast, was a wealthy, thriving city. However, they had a long-standing problem with their water supply. To the north, there were healthy hot springs. To the south, there were clean cold springs. But the water in Laodicea was a mixture of both, tepid and often a carrier of disease. Jesus compared their water to a tepid, sick faith, a result of their complacency caused by their wealth. They felt totally self-sufficient and thought that they didn't need Jesus in their lives.

Jesus instead counselled them to look for gold, clothing, and healing from him. The gold was true wealth, not earned from exploitation of others, but a wisdom for all to live in harmony. The white robes, as in the letter to Sardis, signified faith untainted by idol worship. The ointment was to heal their eyes so that they could see and understand the true way of Jesus Christ. Jesus called to them with a broken heart, asking them to repent. He was knocking at their door, waiting for an answer so that he could come and fellowship with him.

Both of these churches had turned away from the true meaning of Jesus Christ. Sardis had perverted his word until who they worshiped was no longer recognizable, but instead was merely an idol.

When we read the Gospels and are told to love our enemies, care for the poor, and welcome the stranger, are we shocked and surprised by the demands that Jesus makes on people of faith? If so, perhaps we have made Jesus into something easier, something more palatable. Like the church in Laodicea, do we depend on ourselves and our own resources instead of calling out to the Lord? Perhaps our faith has become lukewarm like those of the Laodiceans.

The wonderful message of these passages, though, is despite our failings, Jesus waits at the door, asking to be let into our hearts. All we need to do is to repent and turn back to his true word and let him be our anchor and strength.

Lord, open my heart to who you are! May you be my strength and my rock. Amen.

Joshua 24:14-15

Revere and Serve the Lord

Why is a choice to revere and serve God a daily decision?

The Book of Joshua tells the story of the Hebrew people as they claimed the Promised Land. This passage comes toward the end of the book when the people decided how they would structure their new life in the land they'd conquered, especially spiritually.

Some of the people Joshua spoke to in this passage had been residents in the land before the Hebrews and had worshiped other gods. The Hebrews saw that their neighbors didn't limit their worship to only one deity. Different gods were believed to have different powers; and to many, it just seemed pragmatic to give some allegiance to these specialized gods as well as continuing to worship Yahweh.

Joshua called them all together to speak to them about their worship. The site was Shechem, an important place in the history of the Hebrew people. God first spoke to Abraham at Shechem. Joseph was buried near there. But most importantly, Shechem was where Jacob told his family to "get rid of the foreign gods you have with you" (Genesis 35:2). Jacob held a ceremony in Shechem where his family buried their idols and left them forever.

And so it was fitting that Joshua asked the Hebrew people to consider their own loyalty to God at Shechem. His call to faithfulness was focused on two words: "revere" (or "fear" in some translations) and "serve" (Joshua 24:14). Joshua told the people that proper reverence to the Lord was devotion that recognized the full power and majesty of God. It meant taking their commitment to God seriously. This would absolutely prohibit sharing any devotion between Yahweh and any other deity.

"Serve" in this passage has the same root as *slave* or *servant* and means exclusive, wholehearted commitment. Joshua announced to the people that while they had the choice of whom they would serve, he and his family were committing themselves to the Lord.

Deuteronomy 6:5 says, "Love the LORD your God with all your heart, all your being, and all your strength." This verse, known as the greatest commandment, is the *Shema*. Devout Jews affix a capsule called a *mezuzah* to their doorposts and put inside of it a piece of paper with this verse printed on it. Its purpose is to remind them of their pledge to revere and serve God. That's because a choice to serve the Lord isn't made once and then forgotten. Instead it's an active, ongoing choice to be faithful to God every moment of every day.

The world will compete for our loyalty, but God demands to be first priority. The *mezuzah* is a beautiful reminder for Jewish people of this daily decision to put God first. Christians don't have a single physical reminder like the *mezuzah* to reinforce our commitment to the Lord, but this commitment is at the very heart of our faith. Every new day is a new commitment to revere and serve the Lord for the faithful.

As for me and my house, I will serve you, O Lord. Amen.

Serving a Demanding God

How can we meet the challenge of reverence and service that God demands?

Joshua challenged the Hebrew people at Shechem to make a decision about whom they would worship and told them that following Yahweh would demand reverence and service. Immediately, the people responded as a force that they would choose to follow the Lord.

Although they were a generation removed from those who experienced the Exodus, they remembered God's grace and protection for their forebearers who were rescued from Egypt and made the harrowing journey. They were grateful to God for driving out their enemies from the Promised Land. They had heard of God's mighty works and they were thankful. They unambiguously declared their devotion and chose to worship the Lord.

Reading further, you'll see Joshua's puzzling response. He told the people that they could not serve the Lord "because he is a holy God. He is a jealous God. He won't forgive your rebellion and your sins" (Joshua 24:19). Joshua was certain that they would not be committed enough to follow through on their promise. To take a commitment like this lightly meant that they were flirting with angering the almighty God of all Creation. Joshua warned them if they pledged themselves to God, apostasy would not be forgiven. Their commitment must be certain and unshakeable.

The people assured Joshua that they would serve and obey God. Significantly, verse 24 literally reads that they would "listen to his voice." This is important because it stresses that they were committing themselves to a relationship. They were expecting a connection with God in which, with God's help and guidance, they could respond in obedience. It meant that this promise wasn't just one-sided. God would speak to them and direct them in their faith.

Like the letter to the church at Laodicea in the Book of Revelation, this was a wake-up call to lukewarm faith. Joshua told the assembled people that it was better not to worship God at all than to worship halfheartedly. Committing ourselves to the Lord means to give our lives to God, nothing less.

Every congregation and every individual in every congregation needs to ask themselves how committed they are to the Lord. Reverence and service on the scale required by God is constant and demanding. Failure means disrespecting the Creator of the cosmos. How can we possibly live up to these requirements?

The answer is in the translation of verse 24: "We will listen to his voice." Because we are in a relationship with the holy God, we are guided by God and God's *hesed*, everlasting love. Committing ourselves to God isn't just following a code of ethics and going to weekly worship. It's entering into a relationship that demands daily connection with God's guidance through prayer and seeking God's will in everything we do.

Lord, may I listen to your voice. Guide me in your love. Amen.

Joshua 24:25-28

Reminders of the Lord

What reminds you of your commitment to God?

My husband and I travel all over the world and have spent long periods of time in many countries. One of the things I love about being in a country with a Muslim population is the call to prayer. Five times a day, the undulating tones of the *muezzin*, the official who sings the *salat*, break into the routine of the day, reminding each person of the power and love of God, and also the commitment each person has made to the Lord. Five times a day, people who are faithful put down whatever else they are doing and turn to praising God.

When I heard the call, I also took the time for my own prayers. When we came back home, I missed the sudden reminders every day of my allegiance to God.

In the United States, many people have physical objects to remind them of their commitment to God. Maybe it's a cross to wear or a picture on the wall. In this passage in Joshua, the people pledged themselves to the Lord, and to remind them of that pledge, Joshua placed a large stone under an oak tree in God's holy place. I imagine they walked by the stone on the way to get water, to go to the market, or to conduct business in town. Every time they saw the stone, they would recall the pledge they made to revere and serve only the Lord. It was their symbol of their covenant with God.

A covenant is a serious, binding commitment. God does not honor a casual faith or worship that fits to the convenience of the follower. If we count ourselves among those who have chosen the Lord when we "choose this day whom we shall serve," it means our lives have changed because the purpose of our lives is now to be devoted to God. It is simply why we are on earth.

The nature of human beings is to become distracted by the minutia of our lives. Before I get up each morning, I think through what is scheduled each day and what I need to get done—the minutia of the day. A better priority would be to focus on God and say a prayer of praise before I even put my feet on the floor. Like the ancient Hebrews on this occasion, I am trying to have reminders throughout my home and daily routine to break through my thoughts to remind me of my commitment to the Lord.

If we have chosen to revere and serve God, then we need to structure our environment, our schedules, and our priorities to reflect that. God needs to be able to intrude on us at any time, and we have to arrange our lives to allow that. That also means listening for God's word throughout the day, open to God's call.

God wants a relationship, and that doesn't happen when we don't hear God. May we always be ready to hear God calling!

Lord, help me to establish daily routines that remind me of my commitment to you. Amen.

A Covenant of Peace

How realistic are the promises in Scripture?

The prophet Ezekiel was born to a family of priests in Jerusalem somewhere around 623 BC. In 597 BC, a large number of the elite citizens from Jerusalem were taken into captivity by the Babylonians, including Ezekiel, who was then about 25 years old. He lived the rest of his life in Babylon as an exiled slave. The Book of Ezekiel is a series of prophecies and visions he had while he lived in Babylon.

The book is divided into three sections. The first relates God's judgment against Israel for her disobedience and apostasy. The second section tells of judgment against other nations. The third, from which today's passage comes, tells of God's salvation for the people of Israel and is a vision of hope and forgiveness.

It's important to remember that this passage was written in the darkest days of ancient Israel's history. Imagine how the Hebrew people reacted when they heard this hopeful prophesy! When things look bad, it can be difficult to believe that life will ever be joyful again. Ezekiel never saw the return of his people to Israel. But even if he had, this prophecy still seems too good to be true.

Read it again, with the eyes of an exiled person. It says the people will obey all of God's decrees. They will have a wise and good king modeled after King David. They will live in peace in an everlasting covenant with the Lord. They will multiply and be strong, and other nations will not dare to attack them because God's presence will be among them. Moses pitched the tent of meeting, God's sanctuary, outside of the camp. But in this prophesy, God will be in their midst, sheltering them under his protective tent. Their relationship with God will be everlasting, happy, and holy.

Ezekiel's vision was eschatological, speaking of the final climax of history when God will come to dwell on earth with God's people. Even today, that vision of a healed, whole earth seems difficult to believe. Hunger, wars, disease, destruction of the environment—so many things currently work against this vision. How can we trust that there will be a future where the world is peaceful, restored, and in accordance to God's holy will? It probably seemed too good to be true for those exiles in Babylon in Ezekiel's time, just as it seems too good to be true today.

But Jesus taught us to pray, "Your kingdom come. Your will be done, on earth as it is in heaven" (Matthew 6:10, NRSV). Ezekiel's vision is exactly what we pray for when we pray the Lord's Prayer. The kingdom of God, come to earth, was the promise of Ezekiel, just as it was the promise of Jesus Christ. It's the hope for the future of humanity, and because it is a hope that runs throughout Scripture, it's a promise we can trust.

Lord, may your kingdom come and your will be done on earth as it is in heaven! Amen.

Jeremiah 31:31-34

A Second Chance

What does "a new covenant" mean in the Book of Jeremiah?

I taught high school in a program called "Saving 9." Statistics show that if students fail ninth grade, the probability of them dropping out of school skyrockets. "Saving 9" identified students in the second half of the school year who were failing ninth grade and put them together in a new class to give them special attention so they could pass.

The one stipulation was that in order to be accepted into the program, they had to commit to doing the work involved and dedicate themselves to passing. It was demanding for the students because most of them didn't have study skills or know techniques for learning. We had to teach that, too. But once they learned how to learn, most of them succeeded and went on eventually to graduate. "Saving 9" gave those students a second chance. The program realized they were lacking in basic skills they needed to graduate school, and it helped them to develop them.

The Hebrew people had broken their covenant with God, despite God's love and care. They didn't have the ability to remain faithful and devoted. God gave them a second chance to develop a relationship with God. But, first, God had to teach them how to be successful in a covenant relationship. God had to change their hearts so they were able to take advantage of their second chance.

This new covenant was not new law, but a second chance at keeping the Law, this time with a God-inspired attitude toward obedience. After going through the agony of exile and slavery in Babylon, Israel finally understood the implications of turning away from the Lord. God began the process of reconciliation by forgiving them and bringing them back into God's care.

This was not the first time God had forgiven this sinful people. These were the people whose ancestors had danced around the golden calf in the wilderness. They had worshiped Canaanite deities when they arrived in the Promised Land. Over and over, they had disobeyed the Lord. But this time, they could be hopeful because God would change their hearts and motivate them to obedience. God promised to turn them in the right direction when they could not do it themselves.

As Christians, we equate the new covenant with Jesus Christ. Jesus' dramatic destruction of the hold of sin and death on us all surely was a radical re-creation of the relationship between God and humanity. But it is important to realize that all throughout history, God redefined the relationship with the people to enable a new understanding, new healing, and new connection. God was and always has longed to repair broken relationships with those God loves.

Lord God, thank you for your amazing *hesed*, your everlasting love, and your desire to heal broken relationships with your people. Amen.

A New Relationship

How did the relationship we are able to have with God change through the sacrifice of Jesus?

When I was in seminary, I took a difficult class with a brilliant yet demanding professor. I felt a real chasm between us, and I was constantly working to please her. While I respected her and her knowledge, it was difficult for me to be around her without feeling a bit anxious. She was intimidating, and I often owed her work!

Later in my studies, I was chosen to teach an artist's consortium at the seminary. I was amazed to realize the professor who had been so intimidating to me was interested in enrolling in the program I was teaching! While my program wasn't scholarly, it was incredible to me that our roles had changed. We connected on a new level, not as student and professor, but as two people exploring a creative outlet together.

In this passage, the writer of Hebrews described the relationship the Hebrew people had with God, and then how it had changed once Jesus instituted the new covenant. Hebrews 12:18-21 depicts Mount Sinai, where Moses received the Law. It was an awe-inspiring and terrifying place. There were storms and loud trumpet blasts, but the most frightening thing was the sound of the voice of God. Everyone who approached Mount Sinai came as a sinner, unworthy before the Lord. So while it was a good place, the site of the giving of the Law, it was also a place of fear that emphasized human unworthiness before God.

Although God had forgiven the people over and over again for their sins, it took Jesus Christ to change the basis of their relationship with the Lord. So in verses 22-24, instead of Mount Sinai, the people were called to "Mount Zion, the city of the living God, heavenly Jerusalem" (verse 22). This is the site of the living God, the God of grace and peace. The city is full of thousands of joyful angels and a place of glad reunion with Christians who have died, the firstborn. It's our vision of heaven.

To enter this city of joy, one has to pass through the gateway of the righteous, but it's guarded by our Advocate and Savior, Jesus Christ. Instead of Sinai's harsh judgment, the blood of Christ purifies all who approach him. Instead of a covenant of law, he has instituted a covenant of forgiveness and mercy. The entire relationship with our God has shifted. It's not one of fear and unworthiness, but of love and delight in one another.

Those of us who follow the Lord are blessed by the guidelines and structure of the Law. That has not changed. God's law is the best instruction book for living on this planet. But Jesus takes us beyond the Law to a new realization of grace and forgiveness, a place where we can dance with the angels in God's Holy City.

Lord Jesus, thank you for your sacrifice, the way of entry into the holy city of Zion. May we dance with the angels! Amen.

31

Deuteronomy 29:10-29

Rehearsing the Covenant

Why did Moses have the people re-commit to the covenant before entering the Promised Land?

One of the sports I particularly enjoy watching during the Summer Olympics is the high dive. It's incredible to me how the divers are able to twist and turn their bodies as they fall through space. Just before they leap, many divers pause for a moment. I understand that they are playing out in their minds the movements they will need to do for a successful dive. It's a little mental rehearsal.

In this passage, Moses and the Hebrew people were poised at the entrance to the Promised Land. Many things could go wrong. So Moses paused to speak to them about what they needed to do to make their lives with God in their new home successful. He reiterated the covenant that they had made with the Lord, rehearsing the promises that they had made to be faithful. He wanted to cement those oaths in their mind before they proceeded.

Notice that everyone was included in this covenant, not only the elite or the decision-makers. Children, immigrants, and servants were asked to swear the oath. Verse 15 even included those who weren't present. This covenant would include future generations and encompass every last person, even those who were hanging back in their own hearts. It was impossible to excuse yourself. If you were part of the community, you were part of the covenant. The disobedience of one could poison the entire population.

Many commentators believe that this passage was written during the time that the Hebrew people were returning from the Babylonian exile and then these verses were inserted back into Deuteronomy. These verses would have been relevant each time God's people were on the cusp of entering or re-entering the Promised Land and were reassessing their relationship with the Lord. If they had indeed been written later, then the people had already broken this covenant by worshiping idols and other deities at the time of its authorship. It would have been a harsh reminder of how they had failed the Lord and of the bitter consequences of breaking the covenant.

It takes courage and hope to stand at the edge of a new endeavor, especially when you have failed before. By reviewing the covenant with the people and making them aware of God's displeasure if they should be disloyal, Moses caused them to rehearse the importance of their relationship with the Lord as they began a new stage of their lives. He focused on where they might make mistakes so that they would be especially careful not to fail. Moses' rehearsal of the people's covenant with God is a powerful tool that we can use for keeping our relationship strong when we face new events in our lives.

Lord, prod me to pause and recommit myself to you, especially when there is change in my life. Amen.

Why 99-Year-Olds Run

What moves you to act in an extravagantly generous manner?

You don't ordinarily imagine someone almost 100 years old lacing up their athletic shoes and running as fast as they can. The opening verses of Genesis 18, though, paint such a picture. Abraham was bursting with the energy of a 20-year-old. "As soon as" three strangers appeared, he "ran from his tent to greet them" (Genesis 18:2).

Showing hospitality to strangers was a mandate in the ancient world (Leviticus 19:33-34). Abraham, though, went well beyond the minimum requirements. An offer of bread turned into a full-course meal. Additionally, he raced to prepare it, as if he couldn't wait to serve them. When he did offer the food, he stood to the side as if he were a servant, attending to their needs.

Why the hurry and the extravagance? There is no indication that Abraham knew the strangers had divine roots, nor that he was seeking a favor. Although the text begins with "the LORD appeared" (Genesis 18:1) it quickly turns into the plural, "three men" (verse 2). The sense is that they would eventually reveal themselves to be angels (19:1), bringing with them the divine presence.

Perhaps the reason behind Abraham's urgent generosity lay in the kinship he felt with the strangers. He knew what it was like being a wanderer. He'd left home six chapters earlier in Genesis, at the age of 75. He knew the vulnerabilities and needs of an alien. He also knew the possibilities of seeing people and things in new ways, not bound by traditions, habits, and histories.

So, he was overjoyed at the opportunity to care for these men. It's reminiscent of the compassion of the good Samaritan (Luke 10:25-37).

The side effect of such joy-produced hospitality was the announcement that Sarah would have a child. A closer reading suggests that if he hadn't offered friendliness to keep the men from passing by (Genesis 18:3), he and Sarah wouldn't have received the promise of a child at that time.

All strangers have the potential to be bearers of God's presence. We may fear them, since they are different from us. But Abraham's joy at the possibility of serving unknown aliens is foundational. It has been, and continues to be, the model for people of faith: "Don't neglect to open up your homes to guests, because by doing this some have been hosts to angels without knowing it" (Hebrews 13:2).

Like Abraham, the abundance of our hospitality is in direct proportion to the joy we have in serving the visitor. In the process, although we don't seek it, we receive a blessing in return. In our welcoming the stranger, we receive new perspectives, possibilities, and relationships.

Through sharing our abundance, God's dreams for the future unfold.

Lord, please give me eyes to see you in the faces of others, a heart to bless them, and fast feet to serve them! Amen.

Deuteronomy 23:24-25

The Tension Between Taking and Giving

How do you balance taking care of your needs while being considerate of the needs of others?

You're hungry as you stand in the front of the line at a potluck meal. What do you do? Fill your plate? Or do you take less, so everyone will have enough? On a larger scale, this is similar to a situation the Hebrews faced as they coalesced into a nation.

Deuteronomy contains the speeches Moses made at the end of the Hebrews' 40-year wilderness wandering. They were farewell words of instruction to this community. The Jews were about to begin their journey into the Promised Land led by Joshua, Moses' successor.

His teachings today are in a section (Deuteronomy 23:15–25:19) meant to guide the people in their relationship with God and with one another. They detail specific, practical instances of community life that could result in conflict if not handled properly.

Today's verses anticipate a fellow Israelite going into a neighbor's vineyard or grain field. Like you in the buffet line, this person is hungry. Moses' counsel is that the person may take and eat, but just enough for his immediate needs. No basket for additional grapes and no sickle for more grain.

Two principles lie behind this. The first is affirming abundance for all. A hungry person may go into someone else's field since the fruits of the earth are God's unrestricted gifts. The owner of the land is simply a steward and must, accordingly, welcome a hungry brother or sister. The early Christians would echo this centuries later when "none of them would say, 'This is mine!' about any of their possessions, but held everything in common" (Acts 4:32).

The second principle is showing respect for the provider. The hungry person must consider the needs and rights of the field's owner. If the person takes too much, and others do as well, then the owner and his family may be in need. This would then be the same as stealing. Hebrew society must be based upon such mutuality of shared abundance.

Ultimately, personal habits should reflect communal responsibility. Mutuality ensures that everyone has enough. When both parties respect the needs of others, then abundance is assured. There will be sufficient food for the planter as well as the stranger. The community will also be strengthened because, like the early church, no one will be in need.

The "What's in it for me?" mentality undercuts God's vision for the community. It gives rise to withholding from the needy out of greed and fear. Likewise, taking without gratitude and respect is also sinful.

True mutuality requires giving up a sense of entitlement. But strengthening relationships, helping the needy, and glorifying God yield an abundance of satisfaction.

God, thank you for the gifts from the land that sustain me, and for those who generously share those gifts. Amen.

Mark 8:1-10

A Miracle's Difficult Lesson

How do you develop an outlook that seeks abundance for all?

Type "How long does it take to start a new habit?" into your internet search engine, and you'll get a variety of answers. All sources agree, though, that it takes an extended period of time. The disciples demonstrate this difficulty in today's passage. How long would it take them to begin looking at life from a new perspective?

While all four Gospels include the story of Jesus feeding the 5,000, only Mark and Matthew (Matthew 15:32-39) describe a later, subsequent time when he fed 4,000. Comparing the two incidents reveals a key difference. In the 5,000 feeding, Jesus began by asking the disciples to provide food for them. In the 4,000 feeding, though, he simply noted that the crowd was hungry. It's as if he was testing them. Had they learned from the previous miracle, that when you're around Jesus, anything can happen, even a miraculous meal?

They hadn't. Their pessimistic response in Mark 8:4 reflects their habit of assuming a scarcity framework. Jesus would mildly criticize them later for their lack of understanding and faith (verses 17-21). It would take time for them to live into the belief that when you were with Jesus, the old limits of scarcity and pessimism no longer applied.

Comparing the two feeding miracles in Mark points to a way Christians can move ahead more faithfully. In both accounts (6:34; 8:2), Jesus initiated the miracles because of compassion. The Greek word for this term conveys a sense of extremely strong emotion, of feeling an inward compulsion to act on behalf of someone. It's as if the depth of his compassion resulted in the abundance produced in the miracles; people weren't just satisfied, but there were baskets full of leftovers.

Similarly, when the disciples allowed themselves to be moved as forcefully by compassion as the Master was, they would be able to anticipate abundant possibilities instead of being restricted by a scarcity mentality.

The importance of compassion is underscored by the setting for today's event. When Jesus fed the 5,000, he was ministering in an area close to his home; his audience was Jewish. In today's text, though, he was traveling in the region of the "Ten Cities" (7:31), a predominantly Gentile area. Jesus' compassion knows no human distinction. The needs of Jew and non-Jew alike moved him equally as well as deeply.

When we love beyond human distinction, we will be well on our way to developing the habit of trusting in God's abundance. As a result, miracles will happen.

Jesus, I pray for a heart that is moved by the needs of others. Encourage me to act on their behalf, trusting your power. Amen.

The Joy Behind the Second Pentecost

How do you find freedom from being married to your possessions?

Many financial planners start with the commonsense maxim, "Pay yourself first." When you get your paycheck, set back a certain portion of it for needs and long-term goals. Discretionary spending starts after that.

The Christians in today's passage, though, would have found such advice puzzling. They sold their possessions and, instead of saving, put everything into a fund that supported others. They did this freely and joyfully. Looking more closely at the context, we discover they did this because of what we could call a second experience of Pentecost. Acts 2 details when the Holy Spirit first fell upon the believers. That Pentecost narrative concluded with a passage (Acts 2:42-47) similar to the one we read today.

Acts 3:1–4:22 describes Peter and John healing a lame man, being tried for it by the religious authorities, and bearing witness to the gospel. Upon their release, the church prayed, the building shook, and the Holy Spirit filled them with confidence (4:31).

This second Pentecost resulted in uniting the faith community even more tightly. Being "one in heart and mind" (verse 32) conveys the sense of sharing the same feelings and thoughts. It's a unity Paul described as "if one part suffers, all the parts suffer with it" (1 Corinthians 12:26). Such cohesion drives out a divisive "This is mine" mentality.

They could live in this amazing way because their experience of the Holy Spirit validated what they'd witnessed. Christ is present, right here and right now. They had seen him heal a lame man and give confidence to the apostles. Consequently, when those leaders preached the Resurrection, it became a lived reality.

It was impossible to separate being united with Christ from being united with one another. The earthly Jesus had felt the hunger, pain, and loneliness of people. His compassion compelled him to address such need wherever he found it.

Consequently, his followers shared the same compulsion. It would have been an insult to his presence if anyone in the fellowship lacked anything. The early believers did whatever it took to ensure there were no needy people in their midst. Selling what they had and sharing it was a small price to pay for the welfare of a brother or a sister.

Today's passage reflects a maturing church. The early believers had witnessed the grace of Jesus' presence and would continue to be moved by his compassion. Following his example, they would love others so much that giving to them became more important than keeping from them.

The history of the church was written by generous people sensitive to human need. Through such compelling love, they demonstrated that there is abundance for all.

Lord, thank you for loving me so extravagantly! Touched by your presence, inspire me to love others just as generously. Amen.

Developing a "Good Eye"

How do you find happiness in life?

A middle-aged businessman made a confession in his small group at church. "I've climbed the corporate ladder all my life. When I got to the top, I saw that I'd placed the ladder against the wrong house."

His admission could have been included in Proverbs. Part of the wisdom literature in the Old Testament, it reflects on what it takes to live a life that's happy and faithful. The sayings span centuries of Hebrew thought.

Today's passage contains a warning and a promise regarding a person's relationship with wealth. Proverbs 22:7-8 warn of the misuse of power associated with money. The fact that there had to be a prohibition against charging interest on loans to the poor (Exodus 22:25) points to the problems that could arise from the practice. It can tempt a rich person to "sow injustice," including imprisoning those who cannot pay (Matthew 18:22-34). It can also enslave a borrower, fearing such injustice.

The foundation of a happy life regarding money, by contrast, is to be "generous" (Proverbs 22:9). The literal meaning of the Hebrew is "to have a good eye." It conveys the intent behind Jesus' teaching in Matthew 6:22-23. After warning about the destructiveness of greed, he said, "The eye is the lamp of the body. Therefore, if your eye is healthy, your whole body will be full of light."

A person with healthy eyes sees God's abundance everywhere and delights in sharing instead of hoarding. He or she will seek ways to help others with what they've been given. They are compelled by a spirit of generous compassion.

The surest sign of such a happy person is how they relate to the poor. The Hebrew writer goes so far as to say they're happy because they give food to the hungry. This differs from the spirit of the wealthy young man in the New Testament, who went away sad because Jesus invited him to give generously to the impoverished (Matthew 19:16-22).

Giving food to the poor is more personal than simply giving money. Providing a meal, in addition to addressing a physical need, also provides an opportunity for connecting. Sharing food breaks down barriers and promotes justice, a key theme running throughout the Old Testament. It will culminate in the New Testament when Jesus' compassion provides a final meal.

Discipleship requires good eyesight. Ordering our lives along the lines of generous kindness ensures that there will be enough for all of God's people. It will also give us the assurance that we've put our ladder against the right house.

Lord of compassion and generosity, open my eyes to see the good waiting to be done all around me today. Amen.

John 21:9-13

John's Last Word

If you summed up your mission as a disciple, what would you write?

Have you ever read a captivating book that had a great conclusion, then discovered it had an epilogue? It's as if that one last chapter was so important the author just couldn't omit it. It had to be included so as to leave the reader with a final, gripping thought.

John 21 forms such an epilogue. It presents the remarkable scene of Jesus inviting the apostles to breakfast. This meal resembles a private, more intimate version of his feeding of the 5,000 in Chapter 6. Not only is the menu the same, but John's description of him giving the food to his disciples (21:13) is almost identical to how he distributed it to the crowd (6:11).

It's in the unique elements in the epilogue that we discover John's intent. Instead of a couple of fish (6:9), there were 153 "large" ones at this breakfast (21:11). The disciples hauled in this catch, without losing a single fish, by following Jesus' command. Additionally, instead of five loaves of barley, the bread of the poor, there were simply loaves of bread.

The entire meal had thus been upgraded. The disciples had a hand in producing it because of their trust in Jesus and were thoroughly enjoying it.

John also includes in his epilogue a sense of mystery. Why didn't the disciples recognize Jesus at first, either by face or voice? As in the Emmaus Road story (Luke 24:13-35), the place of revelation for believers is the dining table. When his followers gather in his name and share a meal, their eyes will be opened to his presence and their hearts opened to his instruction.

The message Jesus conveyed comes home in the verse following the breakfast scene. "When they finished eating, Jesus asked Simon Peter, 'Simon son of John, do you love me more than these?' Simon replied, 'Yes, Lord, you know I love you.' Jesus said to him, 'Feed my lambs'" (John 21:15).

The disciples would have gotten the point. Just as Jesus had fed them, so now were they to go and feed others. They were to do so with Jesus' gentle spirit. They were his children, and they would feed his lambs. From now on, they would provide an abundant meal to all who gathered in his name.

The early Christians, reading this epilogue, would have witnessed how this mission unfolded. No one was hungry or in need within their fellowship. Hearts touched by Jesus' love shared what they had generously. They made sure everyone had a place at the table and that the table overflowed with food comparable to warm bread and large fish.

It's good that John included an epilogue. He leaves us with a question that should focus our discipleship: How are we tending to Jesus' lambs?

Master, you call me your child and lovingly provide for me. Similarly, give me grace to care for your lambs, whoever and wherever they are. Amen.

John 6:1-15

Phrases Jesus Never Used

Do you live with an outlook of scarcity or abundance?

Jesus feeding 5,000 is the only miracle he performed that's recorded in all four Gospels. Comparing John's account to the other three (Matthew 14:13-21; Mark 6:32-44; Luke 9:10-17) reveals interesting differences.

Being the last one written, John's narrative reflects the early church's understanding of this miracle's importance. His introduction to the story contains one of the most unique insights. Unlike the other accounts, John interprets Jesus' question to Phillip as a "test" (John 6:6). Would the disciple respond with trust in Jesus' power? It was a question the early Christians, faced with daunting problems, would have asked themselves.

Phillip's response started sarcastically. Should we spend half a year's salary for a picnic? It ends pessimistically. Even if we spent so much, "there wouldn't be enough for each person to have just a little bit" (verse 7). Andrew reinforced the pessimism. After noting the bread and fish, he interjected rhetorically, "But what good is that?" (verse 9).

The rest of the story teaches that "just a little bit" and "What good is that?" were never in Jesus' vocabulary. Everything he did from that point on was a lesson in miraculous abundance.

John notes that the bread and fish Jesus used were from a child or a young teen (verse 9). He may be implying that such a person would not have shared the adults' pessimism. Additionally, the youth may have come from a poor family, since barley bread was the food of common people, being cheaper than wheat. That would have made the offering even more impressive.

The remainder of the narrative relates what happens when even a small gift is placed in Jesus' hands. In contrast to each person not even having a little bit, everyone had "as much as they wanted" (verse 11). When Jesus assigned the Twelve to pick up the leftovers, it's as if he wanted to impress this lesson upon them. Filling so many baskets, when they had started with not enough food for even one, would cause them to think twice before answering any future question from Jesus!

The challenge for modern Christians, as well as for those reading this narrative in the first century, is trusting in a power greater than our own. If we think it is all up to us and our meager resources, then we will paralyze ourselves with "But what good is that?" The image of baskets overflowing with food should be enough for us never to withhold a possible miracle because of fear.

In those situations in which we assume scarcity, Jesus sees abundance. Will we be Phillip and Andrew or the young person with barley loaves and fish?

Master, you took the small and humble and nourished thousands. Open my heart and eyes, so that you may continue filling baskets today. Amen.

8

1 Samuel 28:20-25

Compassion That Transcends Differences

When have you been surprised by unexpected kindness?

The tragic story of King Saul seeking a medium presents difficulties to the modern reader. First, it has a Halloween element in it. The graphic image of a ghost rising from the grave seems more tabloid-like than biblical. Second, it depicts Yahweh as unforgiving. Saul's lone sin in 1 Samuel 15 would lead not only to his death, but also to the deaths of his sons. These features reflect the thought and culture of an ancient era. However, they serve as a backdrop for an extraordinary, and timeless, act of compassion.

King Saul feared a formidable Philistine army because he no longer heard God's voice. The biblical writer ascribes this to divine anger. Contributing also was the king's deteriorating mental state, witnessed by his earlier mood swings (1 Samuel 18:10; 19:9). The fact that he sought counsel from a medium in the Canaanite city of Endor reflects his anguish (28:7).

Witchcraft was common in the nations Israel encountered as it moved into Canaan. It was also strictly prohibited for Jews since they viewed it as a lack of trust in God (Deuteronomy 18:14-15). The journey itself to see the medium also shows Saul's desperation. Traveling to Endor would have been risky, requiring a clandestine trip around the encamped Philistine forces.

Our passage today begins with the natural outcome of Saul's hearing the pronouncement of death in battle the next day: He collapsed. It was at this point, though, that the medium, remarkably, offered a meal. Her invitation is striking in four ways.

She didn't have to do it. Her obligation was only a business deal. It would have been in her best interest for him to leave as soon as possible.

She did it persistently. She repeatedly asked him to get up and eat, for his own well-being.

She did it to a foreigner. Saul was a Hebrew, while she was a Canaanite. They shared neither the same culture nor the same deity.

She did it lavishly. Like Abraham addressing his three guests (Genesis 18:1-8), she initially offered "a bit of food." However, also like Abraham, she expended her energy and resources in offering a full meal.

While Saul didn't receive the message he sought, he did receive a supper offered out of compassion. It was a kind, heartfelt gift.

The takeaway is that mercy transcends our differences. Regardless of political, religious, or other distinctions, a person's suffering can move strangers to act as friends.

The medium's persistence in offering the meal serves as a model of compassion. Perhaps the sincerity and intensity behind the offer were more important than the food itself.

Lord, thank you for the witness of this woman. Grant me grace to show kindness with extravagance and intensity. Amen.

Ruth 2:14-16

The Surprising Harvest of Compassion

When have you seen an act of kindness produce unexpected results?

Attending an English as a Second Language class is a moving experience. Seeing people from around the world trying to learn a strange language in a strange land touches your heart. Ruth's story elicits similar warmth. Hers is especially poignant because she became an immigrant not for a better life for herself, but to help her mother-in-law Naomi.

Ruth 1:1-18 provides background for Naomi's plight. Not only did her husband die, but also her only two sons. While she insisted that her two daughters-in-law return to their families and find new husbands for themselves, Ruth refused. She would leave her own family in Moab and journey with her back to Judah, Naomi's birth country.

Like many immigrants, Ruth found herself in a vulnerable position. She became a gleaner, meaning that she followed those who harvested barley, picking up the droppings. Her decision to accompany Naomi left her desperate, but her compassion was noticed and elicited compassion as well.

Boaz, the owner of the field, heard of Ruth's remarkable journey (Ruth 2:11). That prompted him to offer a bounty of generosity and kindness. Of the many thoughtful things he did, the most striking was displayed around the lunch table.

Today's text finds Boaz going well beyond providing only food. He gave Ruth the status of equality by insisting that she sit with the harvesters as she dined. Such an act transcended the socioeconomic prejudice of a lower-class gleaner sitting with the harvesters. Also, more importantly, it transcended the Jewish prejudice against Gentiles.

This story, taking place early in Israel's history during the time of the judges, reflects a theme running throughout Scripture. A person is judged by the quality of the heart, not by his or her nationality or status. The Moabites were ancient enemies of the Jews (Numbers 22:1-21), but Ruth's character shone with a purity and goodness that was the Jewish ideal.

The story also reveals that the consequences of compassion run deep. Even though Ruth may have had fearful moments, her unwavering support of Naomi touched her neighbors. Boaz modeled this, looking past her immigrant status and welcoming her fully.

God works through people moved by such compassion. The union of Ruth and Boaz, which would have never occurred without her loyalty to her mother-in-law, affected Israel's history. She would become the great-grandmother of King David. She would also be honored as one of only four women mentioned in Jesus' lineage (Matthew 1:5).

Lord, thank you for compassionate people like Ruth and Boaz. Help me notice them, honor them, and learn from them. Amen.

Loving Even When You Don't Feel Like It

Why should you show kindness to your enemies?

There is an unfortunate stereotype that the Old Testament focuses on judgment, while the New Testament emphasizes forgiveness. The Hebrew Scriptures, however, were written over a period of centuries and contain a rich diversity of thought. Proverbs, with its many sayings from Jewish teachers, provides a window through which to see this diversity. Today's verses, centering on relationships, present reflections that connect directly with the gospel.

Jesus taught that words are an indicator of what's in the heart (Matthew 15:18), and James instructed us to "tame" the tongue (James 3:1-12).

Similarly, the Hebrew writer says that right words are "gold apples in a silver setting" (Proverbs 25:11). He wrote from a practical standpoint. The proper choice of words mends relationships and provides insight. How much better for words to be used instead of swords, since a "tender tongue can break a bone" (verse 15).

Proper speech, though, must be backed up by proper actions. In contrast to an ancient world where retribution was often the norm (Deuteronomy 19:21), the writer closed by focusing on kindness. Giving an enemy food and drink is a concrete way of obeying Jesus' command to love your foe. Bread and water are foundational for life, and offering them is a way of wishing health and wholeness for someone. Showing such compassion also invites healing in the relationship.

The phrase "heap burning coals on their heads" (Proverbs 25:22) may refer back to Proverbs 25:4. Refining silver entails heating the metal to remove impurities. Similarly, the act of kindness elicits a response from the enemy. Will that person be moved by it? Will it begin a melting away of differences or hostilities, so a positive relationship may emerge?

There is, of course, no guarantee of resolution. Regardless, like choosing not to use antagonizing words, the offer of food and drink undercuts the defenses of an enemy. That person must decide whether to pursue a zero-sum game of win/lose or to let the person's kindness open the door for understanding and reconciliation.

Centuries after the Jewish writer advocated for this higher road, Paul quoted him almost exactly. He then concluded with, "Don't be defeated by evil, but defeat evil with good" (Romans 12:21).

The standard for the modern Christian, as for the ancient Jew, is the same. Offering food and drink to an enemy shows that we are serious in being "complete in showing love to everyone" (Matthew 5:48).

Master, thank you for showing me the higher path of love. Help me reach out to those who, at first, may seem unlovable. Amen.

11

Romans 12:17-21

The Key to Peaceful Living

What must happen if you are to live peacefully with others?

It was one of those church meetings.

Leaders were debating whether to undertake a new, resource-intensive project. The discussion grew heated, and emotions flared. Finally, one person, who had been quiet, spoke. In a low-key manner, he recapped both sides of the argument, outlined why he thought the pros outweighed the cons, and volunteered to help lead the project if the council approved it.

His speech dramatically changed the atmosphere. Members came together, put aside differences, and moved ahead positively. He demonstrated Paul's admonition in today's passage: "To the best of your ability, live at peace with all people" (Romans 12:18). He achieved such a difficult task by embodying what Paul wrote a few verses earlier (verses 9-17).

Today's reading is part of a section where Paul wrote with a style and substance similar to Jesus' Sermon on the Mount (Matthew 5–7). The apostle listed a series of imperatives focused on how a Christian must live out a redeemed lifestyle in relating to others—believers and nonbelievers.

Leading up to instructing us not to repay evil with evil (Romans 12:17, 19), Paul graphically defined *humility*: "Consider everyone as equal, and don't think that you're better than anyone else" (verse 16).

Such a quality is a non-negotiable prerequisite for everything he wrote in this text. Specifically, a humble person refrains from hurting an enemy for two reasons.

First, such a person will "show respect for what everyone else believes is good" (verse 17). Such "good" builds up the community and seeks an inclusive fellowship; this contrasts with the ego-driven duality of friend/foe. The positive qualities he listed in verses 9-15, such as loving genuinely and blessing those who harass you, take root only in a humble heart.

Second, humility leaves room for God to be the judge. If there is to be wrath, it must come from one who judges another's heart better than we do. As Jesus taught in Matthew 7:1-5, our own flaws make flawless judging impossible.

Better than prideful vengeance is humble kindness. Paul appropriately quoted Proverbs 25:21-22. As we noted in yesterday's reading, the burning coals image refers to burning off impurities, as in refining silver. Showing consideration for an enemy may result in that person's transformation, along with the transformation of the relationship. That, in turn, will enable an open-table fellowship to flourish.

Paul concluded the section with the triumphant call to overcome evil with good. Humble people will do that, and thus inherit the earth by treating enemies as friends.

Master, as you walked among us with gentleness and kindness to all, so also may my steps be measured with yours. Amen.

The Reward of Loving Enemies

How do you feel when you show undeserved kindness to someone?

In *The Gentle Art of Blessing*, Pierre Pradervand writes of the resentment he felt at being forced out of a job. His unfair treatment consumed him daily until Jesus' teaching about loving and praying for enemies stopped him.

Pradervand immediately began blessing those who had mistreated him. He sincerely wished for them the best in all aspects of their lives. As he practiced this daily, such blessing moved from an exercise to a genuine expression from his heart. This freed him for living a richer, deeper life.

This sincerity on behalf of an enemy is what the author of 1 Peter had in mind in his instructions to the early Christians. He wrote to encourage them to endure the fierce persecutions they were suffering. While there is uncertainty as to which those were—Nero's in 64 AD or later ones—the mistreatment the believers felt was intense. They were reviled, tortured, and killed.

Peter expressed his hope that Jesus would return to deliver them: "You share his suffering now so that you may also have overwhelming joy when his glory is revealed" (1 Peter 4:13). The more immediate source of hope, though, was the strength the Christians discovered in how they conducted themselves.

Peter reminded them of how Jesus handled his persecution: "When he was insulted, he did not reply with insults. When he suffered, he did not threaten revenge. Instead, he entrusted himself to the one who judges justly" (1 Peter 2:23).

It was essential for the Christians to demonstrate this, first, with one another. The beginning of this is to be "of one mind" in Christian fellowship, as Peter stated in today's text. He listed the qualities of such an intimate fellowship. Anchored in humility, they reflect how Jesus lived.

In 1 Peter 3:9, Peter said that this type of living would carry over to the very people who were hurting and killing them. He noted that persecution comes in deed ("evil") and word ("insult"). Regardless, the believer's response is to give a blessing.

The Greek word for "blessing" literally means "a good word." For the Christian, a good word is that which expresses sincere concern for the enemy. It's praying for them, wishing them well, advocating for them, forgiving them, and not letting them anger you.

Through demonstrating a love similar to Christ's, Christians will discover an abiding joy and strength. They will also be making a statement that will offer hope to others oppressed in an immoral, violent world.

While Peter's words are in the form of instruction, we should view them as an invitation. He invites us to live a life that transcends present difficulties. Gently blessing leads to fully living.

Lord, move my heart so that I love my enemy because I want to, not because you told me to. Amen.

Luke 19:1-10

The Mission of Surprising Grace

How can you surprise sinners with unconditional love?

The theme of divine surprise never grows old. From the classic movie *Oh, God!* to TV shows such as *God Friended Me*, an invitation from the Almighty disrupts people's lives in interesting ways. Zacchaeus's surprise encounter with Jesus fits this category. It contains three dramatic elements.

Curiosity. Zacchaeus is the only person in the New Testament described as a "ruler" of tax collectors (Luke 19:2). Tax collectors were reviled because they collaborated with the Romans in taking revenue from their fellow Jews, charging commission in so doing. Someone in charge of them, overseeing their greed and profiting from it, was doubly hated. Such a calloused man, though, was curious about Jesus; perhaps he had heard of him socializing with tax collectors and even calling one of them, Levi, to be a disciple (Luke 5:27-32).

Shocked happiness. To invite someone to a meal reflected honor and possibly friendship. Jesus inviting himself to Zacchaeus's house showed respect to a person everyone else thought was undeserving. The tax collector's quickness to welcome him reflects the surprised joy of being deemed so worthy.

A changed heart. Zacchaeus's speech demonstrated an inner change. In contrast to the rich man who went away sad at the command to give to the poor (Luke 18:18-23), the tax collector gave spontaneously. Additionally, paying someone four times the amount he was overcharged shows a serious desire to obey Jewish law (Exodus 22:1).

Throughout this encounter, Jesus added to the drama by focusing on Zacchaeus. When he invited himself to the tax collector's house, he ignored the hostile crowd, where everyone grumbled (Luke 19:7). When he proclaimed Zacchaeus to be a valued son of Abraham, he addressed the audience but remained looking at him (verse 9).

While this dramatic passage shows the transformation that happens when someone encounters unconditional love, it ultimately points to the mission of Jesus and his church. His calling to seek and save the lost connects to what he said to the Pharisees in an earlier incident involving a tax collector: "I didn't come to call righteous people but sinners to change their hearts and lives" (Luke 5:32).

Other religious leaders viewed people like Zacchaeus as sinners and ignored them. Jesus saw them as beloved children of his Father and reached out to them. The church he would form would be that of the reconciled sitting around a table filled with respect and friendship. For many, that would start with a surprising encounter of grace.

Lord, thank you for inviting yourself into my life. Help me surprise others with your invitation, welcoming them as brothers and sisters. Amen.

1 Samuel 25:2-39

A Blueprint for Being a Peacemaker

How do you help people resolve a conflict peacefully?

When two nations feud with each other, a situation may spark a conflict that can have disastrous consequences. Perceived slights have sometimes resulted in violence that could have been avoided had diplomacy been given a chance.

On a personal level, today's passage describes a situation between two men that could have ended tragically. Fortunately, the action of a wise woman averted disaster.

The dispute started with Nabal rejecting David's request for food. In that culture, this was the same as wishing death on someone. He then added an insult by inferring that Saul was the rightful king, while David held the status of a slave.

David reacted by declaring war. Rage blinded his thinking, leading to a nonsensical vow to avenge a verbal insult by murderous action. He would slaughter not just Nabal, but his innocent male relatives. If he had gone through with his plans, he would have been acting more foolishly than the wealthy man.

Abigail prevented this calamity in an amazing way. In so doing, she gives us a blueprint for making peace. She saw the situation clearly. She understood that David's response would literally be overkill. She also knew that vengeance is God's domain (Deuteronomy 32:35).

Abigail took a risk. She was a woman taking the initiative within a patriarchal society. She was undercutting what her husband had done, and doing so secretly.

Adding to her stress was her knowledge that she would be confronting a future king (1 Samuel 25:28).

Abigail responded generously. The abundance of the food she offered conveyed her wish of abundant life for David. The humble way in which she addressed him underscores this. Such generosity softened David's emotions, opening him to hearing her wise counsel.

A peacemaker enables a person blinded by emotion to step back and regain perspective. David not only repented of his murderous intent but took the high road of not addressing Nabal's slight in any manner. He was content to place the situation in God's hands.

In today's culture of social media that fan the flames of emotions and encourage conflicts, peacemakers are needed more than ever. Abigail's model is extremely timely but also difficult to follow. People who strive to see things clearly, who are willing to take risks, and who respond generously to others may feel as if they are outsiders. But, in the process, they will discover a deeper fulfillment than that which passes for happiness today.

Jesus had the Abigails of this world in mind when he said, "Happy are people who make peace, for they will be called God's children" (Matthew 5:9).

Lord, let your peace flow through me, and let the happiness with which you bless me bless all I meet. Amen.

15

Luke 22:14-20

What Makes the New Covenant New?

When you take Communion, what are you affirming?

The central part of a wedding ceremony is the exchange of promises. Trust that the two people will be faithful to their vows forms the foundation of the marriage covenant.

Similarly, marriage is used in the Old Testament as a metaphor for God's relationship with people (Hosea 2:14-23). The old covenant, through Moses, depended on the Hebrews keeping their vows for the union to endure.

Jesus, at the end of his ministry, talked of a new covenant. He used the setting of the Passover meal as a way to explain and commemorate it. His words in Luke 22:15-16 provide the context for this pivotal supper.

In a phrase unique to Luke, Jesus had "earnestly desired" to eat this meal. This expressed his wish to share food one more time with his beloved friends. However, he was also eager to establish the sacramental meal itself. "Before I suffer" signifies that the dinner would connect to the sacrifice he was about to make on their behalf.

"Fulfilled in God's kingdom" looks ahead to the way this meal would be celebrated after Jesus accomplished his work. It would be a means of relating to him as his disciples lived out their faith.

Jesus emphasized this again in the next verse. "Taking a cup" refers to one of the cups of wine that was part of the Passover meal. He would drink it again, but in a context of a different Passover.

The institution of the Lord's Supper itself, with the breaking of the bread and passing of the cup, follows the order described by Paul (1 Corinthians 11:23-26).

The consecration of the cup contains the key phrase "new covenant by my blood." As the blood of a special lamb was used in the first Passover (Exodus 12:3-7), so would Jesus' sacrifice be central to the new one. This imagery was part of the religious understanding in ancient Israel and sounds foreign to us. However, the new covenant reimagines sacrifice.

Yahweh's bond with us through Moses entailed our obedience to laws and rituals. But the new covenant is based on faith in Jesus' obedience. He obeyed in a way that we cannot. As Paul said later, "He humbled himself by becoming obedient to the point of death, even death on a cross" (Philippians 2:8).

In trusting in what he did, not in what we try to do, we experience a new intimacy with God. Faith in Jesus' obedience fulfills Jeremiah's prophecy (Jeremiah 31:31-34), where God's words are engraved upon people's hearts.

Because of the new covenant, our obedience now comes from a desire to honor God. Taking Communion is a way of expressing our gratitude. It is also a way of embodying a new, inclusive kingdom. As we sit at the table, we affirm our commitment to love God completely and to love our neighbor as ourselves.

Master, accept my life in gratitude for your sacrifice. As you love me so amazingly, so also will I love others. Amen.

The Power of "One Loaf of Bread"

How does taking Communion affect your relationship with others?

What is the setting of your church? Rural, urban, suburban? Where your congregation meets helps shape your understanding of the gospel. It will also present possibilities and problems in living out the good news.

Corinth was a large, prosperous city located in south-central Greece. It was a center of trade, resulting in a diverse population. Additionally, the city hosted a large temple dedicated to the worship of Aphrodite, the Greek goddess of love, beauty, and fertility; Venus is her Roman name.

Paul had this setting in mind when he wrote, "Run away from the worship of false gods!" (1 Corinthians 10:14). This worship featured such immoral practices as cult prostitution. It was also a way of soliciting divine favors, such as protection and procreation.

These actions were so counter to Christian worship and fellowship that the apostle simply asked his readers to stop and think about it. Since they were "sensible," some things should be obvious (verse 15).

When they came together to worship and celebrate the Lord's Supper, Paul pointed to the wine, symbolic of Christ's sacrifice for us. Instead of it being part of a meal people offered to Aphrodite to solicit favors, it is a meal in which believers offer gratitude to Christ for what he did for us on the cross. His unconditional, sacrificial love symbolized in the blood of the new covenant has already blessed us. He's already given us all we need for fullness of life, with God and with one another.

Such worship, focused on gratitude, shapes the Christian fellowship differently when compared to its pagan counterpart. The worship of Aphrodite resulted in catering to the desires of the individuals. However, Christian worship results in bonding together the entire fellowship.

This was Paul's point when he talked about bread after mentioning the cup. In the traditional Communion blessing, the bread is first lifted up, and then the cup (1 Corinthians 11:24-25). In today's passage, though, he places special importance on the communal aspect of the Lord's meal.

Paul mentioned "loaf of bread" three times in these verses. The visual of a single loaf being passed, with each taking a piece, conveys a powerful meaning. The bread, representative of Christ's body, also symbolizes that we are all connected together to his body. We're not individuals seeking our own desires. Instead, we are brothers and sisters to Christ and, like him, ultimately concerned about others' needs first.

Paul used the term *koinonia* to signify this sharing together. It conveys a sense of family that could never be found elsewhere, least of all in the temple of Aphrodite.

Lord, thank you for this family meal. When I take Communion, make me sensitive to the needs of my brothers and sisters around me. Amen.

Exodus 12:1-14

Remembering and Reliving Through a Meal

What makes a meal memorable for you?

Nations mark key events in their past as a way of remembering their heritage and identity. Celebrations around the Fourth of July, for instance, commemorate a focal point in American history.

For ancient Israel, the key event in its history was the deliverance from slavery in Egypt. The celebration of the Passover meal, described in today's passage, commemorates this.

The term itself originates in Exodus 12:12-13. The last plague God visited on Egypt was the killing of the firstborn—human and animal. (The destruction of animals relates to Egyptian idolatry, since animals represented some of their gods.) God would "pass through" Egypt, visiting this destruction on them. However, Yahweh would "pass over" (*Pesach*) the houses of the Hebrew slaves marked by the blood of the sacrificed lamb.

The text contains a mix of instructions for the first Passover and the annual celebration of it. The Hebrews must eat it with their sandals on and fully clothed, ready for a fast escape from Egypt. Their bread was to be unleavened, which was quicker to prepare (Deuteronomy 16:3).

At the same time, reflecting the significance of the event as pivotal for Israel's identity, they should eat the meal with "bitter herbs" (Exodus 12:8), symbolizing the bitterness of their enslavement. Details regarding the lamb, such as observing it for four days, indicate the later importance of offering God the best gift possible.

Verse 14 summarizes the purpose of these instructions. The celebration of Passover is remembering and reliving. The Jews remember that God hears their cries and intercedes powerfully. Their rituals for families to follow in eating the meal (the *Seder*) help them relive Yahweh's saving action on the night preceding the Exodus. Eventually, this would be celebrated nationally through a pilgrimage festival in Jerusalem (2 Kings 23:21-23).

Throughout the millennia of their history, this remembering and reliving has served as a source of hope for the Jewish people. Similarly, the celebrating of the Lord's Supper fulfills this same purpose for Christians.

Rituals that have developed around Communion center on Jesus' words: "Do this in remembrance of me" (Luke 22:19). Taking the bread and cup, like the Jews taking the lamb and the unleavened bread, is a way of reliving that night. It also joins us to generations of believers who've lived the faith before us.

For Jew and Christian, our respective ceremonies must continue forever. The lure of the gods of Egypt, and their modern counterparts, is ever-present. By remembering and reliving, we proclaim our hope in the God who parts seas and opens tombs.

Master, thank you for inviting me to your table. Each time I take the bread and cup, I will remember and be grateful. Amen.

18

Exodus 23:23-25
The Challenge of Trusting God

How do you demonstrate trust in God during a time of crisis?

It's easy for many of us to take food for granted. We buy it prepackaged at the grocery story, several steps removed from the land that produced it. In times of crisis though, such as the COVID-19 pandemic, accessibility to grocery stores and some items was limited. We then realized the importance of the land's bounty, as well as our anxiety when we have limited access to it.

The Hebrews, in their wilderness wandering, were cut off from their food supply in Egypt. They became aware of their reliance upon Yahweh to provide, such as in the provision of manna and quail (Exodus 16).

However, as today's passage notes, when they possessed the land of Canaan, they would become an agricultural nation. How could they be assured that the land would be fertile and that there would be enough water?

Our text is in a section of Exodus called the "Covenant Code." It contains material gathered over a long period of time in Israel's history. Moses' words speak to a timeframe when the nation was already established. They reveal how the Israelites tried to ensure the land's prosperity through idolatry.

The destruction of the Canaanite nations in Exodus 23:23 is linked to the destruction of idols in verse 24. The messenger may refer to the ark of the covenant, the symbol of God's presence and dominance over gods of stone.

Such violence sounds foreign to us. It expresses, though, the passion of the writer in ridding the land of idols associated with the Canaanite nations. He viewed turning to these gods, such as the fertility deity Baal, as an insult to the God who had liberated and cared for the Hebrews. This faithlessness revealed a desire to manipulate these idols instead of trusting in God's love and care. As Moses warns in verse 33, "Don't allow [their gods] to live in your land, or else they will lead you to sin against me. If you worship their gods, it will become a dangerous trap for you."

By contrast, continuing to trust in God's goodness and protection, and consequently obeying the covenant laws, would mean fullness of life. The ground would be as fertile as the sky was when it rained manna and quail. People would be healthy, raise children, and live to an old age.

Unfortunately, Israel did not heed Moses' command to trust and obey. Throughout its history, the prophets would continually call the people to abandon idolatry and renew their covenant with God. Yahweh would continue caring, even in the midst of their turning away. Providing food and water was a tangible sign of a faithful love. Ultimately, God will provide a banquet that will celebrate a new covenant that will be written on their hearts.

God, thank you for being faithful, even when I haven't been. Please empower me to trust you more when I face the unknown. Amen.

When a Meal Forms a Nation

When has a meal helped you find common ground with strangers?

World Wide Communion Sunday can be an especially moving occasion. It connects us in spirit with people from around the globe, providing a powerful backdrop for the sacrament. In today's passage, God invites Israelites to gather periodically from across the land and eat together. Such times would shape their national identity.

Our text begins a section where Moses instructed the Hebrews as to what they must do once they settled in the Promised Land. In the previous chapters, he recapped God's delivering the people from Egyptian bondage and giving basic laws. They were about to end their wilderness journey and become an established nation. How would their relationship with Yahweh and with one another change?

The feasts Moses described would serve three functions:

Unify. Moses started with the command to destroy all Canaanite idols. While this is similar to yesterday's passage from Exodus, there is an emphasis here to destroy "every place" where the idols were worshiped (Deuteronomy 12:2). By contrast, in their new nation, the Israelites should centralize worship in one location (verse 5). This would ultimately be in the capitol of Jerusalem, part of King Josiah's reform (2 Kings 22).

Among the different occasions to gather in that location, the three main Jewish festivals (Deuteronomy 16:1-17) would be central. Those times would visibly demonstrate that no longer did everyone do only "what seems right to them" (12:8).

Celebrate. Abundant food and drink would characterize these gatherings. The offerings people provided showed their desire to share with one another and to praise God for fertile land. Their gifts of grain, wine, olive oil, and meat would provide a lavish meal. They would eat and drink, remembering that "the LORD [had] blessed [them]" (verse 7).

Include. An important part of the banquets would be inclusivity. They would not only be for those who could provide for the banquet. Rather, male and female servants would be included, as would the priests (Levites) who had no land. Moses later specified that some feasts must include immigrants, orphans, and widows (Deuteronomy 16:11).

This inclusion would be central to Israel's identity. It must share God's compassion for those in need. The occasions must reflect the future banquet when God "will prepare for all peoples a rich feast, a feast of choice wines" (Isaiah 25:6).

Christians reading this passage see the connection with the Lord's Supper. As with our Jewish ancestors, we experience the power that comes from joining with fellow believers around a common table. Unity, celebration, and inclusion form our witness to God's continuing involvement in the world.

Lord, thank you for a church that knows no boundaries. Let my life celebrate your unconditional, inclusive love. Amen.

What makes the Lord's Supper special for you?

Occasionally, a person may hesitate in receiving the elements during Communion. This worshiper may feel a sense of unworthiness. As we'll see today, though, Matthew's description of the first Lord's Supper shows how the sacrament is expressly for those who feel unworthy. This comes from how Jesus redefined Passover.

Matthew wrote for a Jewish audience, so his readers were familiar with the Passover ceremony. As we saw in the passage for November 17, the sacred meal celebrates God's deliverance of the Hebrews from slavery in Egypt.

The Gospel writer now shows how Jesus, eating this meal with his disciples, expanded the ceremony's significance. Through the Lord's Supper, Passover will celebrate God's deliverance of all people through the death and resurrection of the Son.

Matthew's account notes that during the meal (the *Seder*) with his disciples, Jesus blessed and passed the bread and cup. He "took . . . , blessed . . . , broke . . . , and gave it to them" (Matthew 26:26). Just as the traditional *Seder* adhered to a ritual, so also would this new Passover meal. Matthew's is the only Gospel where, when Jesus passed the cup, he said that his blood will be poured out "for many so that their sins may be forgiven" (verse 28).

Jesus' blood fulfilled the intent of the covenant God made through Moses. After the Israelites agreed to obey God, Moses took a sacrificed ox's blood and sprinkled it upon the people. He said, "This is the blood of the covenant that the LORD now makes with you on the basis of all these words" (Exodus 24:8).

Jesus now fulfilled what Moses couldn't. His sacrifice binds us to God. He takes away our sins, reconciling us to Yahweh.

Additionally, the covenant will be sustained by him. Jesus said that he wouldn't drink from the cup again until he did it "with you" (Matthew 26:29). This phrase is unique to Matthew, connecting with the Master's final words: "I myself will be with you every day until the end of this present age" (28:20). There is an intimacy between Jesus and his followers that Moses couldn't provide.

Finally, Matthew notes that at the conclusion of the meal, before they left for Gethsemane, Jesus and the disciples sang "songs of praise" (26:30). While these would have been traditional Jewish songs, the early church incorporated singing into worship and daily life. Their songs of praise would give thanks for the love of Christ, who laid down his life so the covenant would be established forever.

Communion is a gift offered and an invitation extended. It isn't focused on what we haven't done, but rather upon what Christ has done, once and for all. Nothing should hold us back!

Master, you invite me to your table out of love. As you gave yourself for me, so do I give myself to you in receiving your bread and cup. Amen.

How aware are you of the needs of those around you during Communion?

The sacrament of the Lord's Supper is central to Christian worship. A fellowship must celebrate Communion with the proper spirit, however. The Corinthian church was not doing this. Paul's instruction to them in today's passage gives timeless guidance. The Corinthians suffered from many internal divisions. First Corinthians 11:17-22 outlines how receiving the Lord's Supper revealed an internal class conflict.

Since Corinth was a prosperous center of trade, the church had wealthy members as well as impoverished ones. Communion took place as part of a larger potluck-style fellowship meal. Since the wealthier members could provide more and better food, they felt entitled to eat that, taking as much as they wanted. It was easy for them to treat this as a private occasion, oblivious to the needs of the poorer participants.

This was so blatantly opposed to the gospel that Paul said it was "necessary" (verse 19) such a division existed, so as to contrast it with a genuine Christian spirit. He did this in verses 23-26, which contain the earliest description of the Lord's Supper. Paul emphasized that the whole meal is sacred, and how we eat it "broadcasts" Jesus' sacrifice (verse 26). He died so that all may be reconciled to God and to one another.

The apostle drew out the practical implications of this in the concluding section. To eat the Lord's meal without regard to the needs of others insults Jesus. Judgment will come upon them just as if they were guilty of shedding his blood. Consequently, Christians must "test" the spirit with which they approach Communion (verse 28). Can each person be mindful of the needs of all who gather, especially those of the poor?

This was a challenge to an already divided fellowship. Paul saw some of the health issues faced by the prosperous members being a judgment on their failure to eat in a worthy manner (verse 30). To avoid a greater judgment would require sacrifice and discipline. Since it was a communal meal rather than a private one, those who had the ability to satisfy their hunger prior to eating together should do so. They should show courtesy and consideration by waiting for all to gather before eating.

What Paul says in this passage provided a real-life situation where Christ's love could be put into action. He challenged a fellowship to transcend socio-economic differences by coming together as a united family around the Lord's Table.

The apostle's words, written almost 2,000 years ago, speak to the church today. We can celebrate Communion inclusively only when we believe that of all the Christian virtues, "the greatest of these is love" (13:13).

Lord, please show me how to honor you by honoring those with whom I share your bread and cup. Amen.

If you received a surprise invitation to a big event, how would you feel?

Inviting people to a party or a wedding can be stressful. How do you determine who should be on the guest list? Social and professional obligations often come into play.

Today's passage recalls a time when Jesus accepted a dinner invitation from a leader of the Pharisees, a strict Jewish sect. He used that setting, and the sense of social obligation, as a backdrop to teach us about God's love and kingdom.

Prior to this event, Jesus showed mercy in healing an ill man on the sabbath (Luke 14:1-6). He then spoke about the importance of humility at a formal meal (verses 7-11). He then took this one step further.

When Jesus instructed his host to invite the "poor, crippled, lame, and blind" (verse 13) to a banquet, he expanded what it means to love your neighbor. He made this point again later in the meal, when he told the parable of a banquet; the same four groups are singled out and invited (verse 21).

God yearns that all, regardless of status, enjoy fullness of life. The marginalized can be overlooked, but not by God. Nehemiah clearly stated this centuries before in giving festival instructions to the people: "Go home and prepare a feast . . . and share it with those who don't have anything: This day is holy to God. Don't feel bad. The joy of GOD is your strength" (Nehemiah 8:10, *The Message*).

Anyone showing such care for the vulnerable will be repaid with this joy of God. Jesus said we will be blessed when we extend such an invitation (Luke 14:14).

Jesus connected this blessing to a future happiness as well. He emphasized that what we do today has consequences tomorrow. He used this as a warning later in Luke, in describing the rich man's fate in ignoring the beggar Lazarus (16:19-31). However, there can be positive results as well. We will receive a more complete joy at the resurrection of the just by inviting the poor to the feast.

The link between the present and the future is the banquet table. A disciple's happiness comes from ensuring that the guest list for today's festival mirrors that for the heavenly one. Practically speaking, today's congregation must resemble tomorrow's.

Early church leaders mandated that all should be warmly invited to the fellowship table. Such nonpartial welcoming was for them, as for us, a way to obey Jesus' teaching in the Sermon on the Mount: "If you love only those who love you, what reward do you have?" (Matthew 5:46).

Our purest form of joy comes from loving as God loves. It's what happens when we expand our guest list and not expect anything in return but a "Yes, I'll come!" response.

Lord, you love beyond human standards. Following your example, empower me to expand my guest list. Amen.

Hungering for Justice and Righteousness

What does God want you to remember, even when you suffer?

Every parent knows the challenges of the toddler phase. A child can say, "I love you!" convincingly. A few minutes later, that same child can throw a memorable tantrum. Hopefully, a toddler will develop to a point where "I love you" is backed up by appropriate actions.

The ancient Hebrews, though, had a difficult time getting to that stage. Today's passage reveals divine frustration and hope. The verses begin with legal language. It's time to "settle" things (Isaiah 1:18). There will be no more claiming to be God's children without acting like it.

In verse 18, God states the case for hope. The parallel format, where the same feeling is expressed twice, shows Yahweh's intense desire to forgive. Sin is scarlet and crimson, the dark colors perhaps signifying blood (verse 15). However, they can be absolved, turning as white as snow and wool.

Isaiah frames each of the following two verses in an "if-then" format. Verse 19 outlines the path to redemption: "If you agree and obey." "Agree" conveys the sincere desire to pursue a more mature relationship with God. It's seeking a righteousness characterized by concrete obedience.

Isaiah specifies what such obedience entails. Verse 17 says, "Seek justice; help the oppressed; defend the orphan; plead for the widow." Furthermore, the leaders must give up bribes so that justice will be available for all (verses 21-23).

This new relationship with God will result in a blessing of the land. It reverses the earlier devastation: "Your land—strangers are devouring it in plain sight. It's a wasteland, as when foreigners raid" (verse 7). Now, when the people hunger for justice and righteousness, the land will be fertile again and they will eat abundantly.

Verse 20, however, outlines consequences if they continue giving lip service to God while ignoring covenantal requirements. As they would eat of the land's bounty, so would they be devoured by invaders. Memories of previous invasions by Assyrians and Babylonians would have still been fresh (2 Kings 16–19).

Today's verses point to the tireless persistence of God never giving up on people, offering them a chance to live into a kingdom where all have a place at the table. Ultimately, Judah would not heed the call, with the resulting Babylonian destruction and exile in 586 BC.

Isaiah, though, also foresaw a time when God's grace would triumph. "Look! I'm creating a new heaven and a new earth: past events won't be remembered; they won't come to mind. . . . Before they call, I will answer; while they are still speaking, I will hear" (Isaiah 65:17, 24).

Anyone with an appetite for a compassionate and just world welcomes such a time.

Holy God, guide my feet, that I may walk in the way of righteousness and along the paths of justice. Amen.

Joel 2:23-26

Hope During a Time of Despair

In what ways may a crisis help you discover God's redeeming presence?

Crises yield opportunities for reflection, repentance, and renewal. The COVID-19 pandemic was a global illustration of this. The sheltering-in-place requirement forced people to look at life outside of their normal routines. Priorities shifted, and sometimes the reset button was pushed.

Joel wrote during a similar time of national peril. Instead of a rampant virus, though, it was locusts. Relentless swarms of differing types (Joel 1:4; 2:25) of these destructive insects had invaded the entire land: "Like blackness spread out upon the mountains, a great and powerful army comes, unlike any that has ever come before them, or will come after them in centuries ahead" (2:2).

The ensuing wasteland devastated the agricultural nation. It was so complete that the land mourned and the animals groaned (1:10, 18). It was a portrait of the Day of the LORD, God's judgment upon the people. Against this bleak backdrop, Joel dared to make a case for hope.

This calamity may serve, "even now," for the people to stop and seek the Lord in more sincere ways (2:12). If they do, they will discover that Yahweh is "merciful and compassionate, very patient, full of faithful love, and ready to forgive" (verse 13). The Lord will become "passionate about this land" and have "pity on this people" (verse 18).

Today's text reflects this through a complete reversal of the devastation. It begins by tenderly addressing the people as "children of Zion" (verse 23). This sets the stage for the grace about to be proclaimed. The Israelites aren't just a nation adhering to commandments. They are, rather, children dependent upon the mercies of their Parent.

A new era will begin with the Lord providing nourishing rains. Such rain was vital if the land was to become fertile and productive again. It was essential that the rain continue throughout the entire season, from planting through harvesting.

God providing such sustained rain will result in filled threshing floors and overflowing vats. Grain, wine, and olive oil symbolized abundant living; these were the elements that had been consumed by the locusts (1:10).

With the plague lifted and the land becoming fertile, the people will eat abundantly once again. Such fullness of life signifies God's presence.

The Day of the Lord, once a label for judgment, will become a day of redemption and reconciliation. God will have "poured out [God's] spirit on everyone" (2:28) as lavishly as water, wine, and olive oil were poured.

Christians see this culminating in God pouring the Holy Spirit onto the church at Pentecost. It's a reminder that a Day of the Lord event is a call for us to open ourselves to the redeeming work of the God who's already here.

Lord, thank you for your faithful love. In times of uncertainty, make me a witness to your abundant, unfailing grace. Amen.

What are your memories of being welcomed home?

Some who celebrate Thanksgiving today will be opening their doors to family and friends. Smiling faces and the aroma of a banquet will greet the guests. It will be an unforgettable scene of welcoming love.

When John wrote Revelation, he was trying to strengthen the first-century Christians who were enduring relentless persecution in the Roman Empire. He wrote today's passage in an effort to lift their eyes from their present suffering and see a future scene of a joyful homecoming.

Our text paints a picture of these Christians being welcomed around God's throne. The verses serve as an interlude during the unsealing of seven scrolls that detail such things as violence, disease, and earthquakes. It is as if, in the midst of such difficulties, John offers a comforting vision of future victory. God will triumph, and no believer will be forgotten.

Revelation 7:9 details a huge, worldwide crowd of believers who have persevered. Wearing white and holding palm branches symbolize purity and victory. They stand in a place of honor, before the throne of God and Jesus, the Lamb. Encircling them are angels and heavenly beings, "the elders and the four living creatures," described in Revelation 4:1-7.

The two songs of praise, one by the Christians who've kept the faith and one by the heavenly beings, show the unity of earth and heaven glorifying God. The angels' song affirms their solidarity with the believers.

Revelation 7:13-14 serves as a transition for John to describe in more detail the identity of the people in white. The elder's description in the remaining verses relies heavily on images from Isaiah. These Christians survived the time of hardship only because of the Lamb. His saving work turned their scarlet clothes to pure white (Isaiah 1:18). From now on, they will be sheltered by God and never hunger or thirst again (Isaiah 49:10). The result will be God drying every tear, because even death has been defeated (Isaiah 25:8).

Such prophetic imagery shows that God's redemptive work is now complete. All the promises made throughout Israel's history have been accomplished through Jesus. The new Passover Lamb has fulfilled the intention of the first one.

John also plays off Psalm 23. The Shepherd is the Lamb in verse 17. He takes away the world's sins (John 1:29) and provides living water (John 7:30-38). He is the only one who can lead the redeemed to the throne of God.

As you give thanks today, remember this scene from Revelation. It is John's portrait of the time when we will hear from the throne, "Welcome home!" What greater reason for thanksgiving can we have than this?

Lord, thank you for your faithfulness. Help me keep warm the hope that will dry every tear and encourage every heart. Amen.

How do you know that Jesus is your Messiah?

Think of John's Gospel as a series of highly dramatized scenes meant to illustrate how Jesus of Nazareth is the Christ (John 20:31). These mini-dramas contain mysterious teachings, antagonists, surprises, and miracles. Interspersed throughout is commentary by the playwright, whom tradition has identified as John the apostle.

The setting for today's scene is near the Temple in Jerusalem. The occasion is the eight-day Festival of Booths (Leviticus 23:33-43). This celebration commemorated God's care for the Hebrew people during their wilderness journey, providing for their needs. Held in the fall, it also became an expression of gratitude for God providing a bountiful harvest.

With this being one of three annual pilgrimages to Jerusalem, many people were gathered that day. Jesus was the topic of conversation. Is he the Messiah or not?

Jesus made a surprise entrance onto the scene midway through the week. Tensions built among him, the crowd, and the religious leaders. Today's passage presents the crescendo, with Jesus returning on the last day of the festival, when worshipers gathered for a large convocation.

One of the rituals that day would have included the ceremonial drawing of water from the nearby pool of Siloam and pouring it in a basin near the altar. This symbolized Moses striking a rock, with a resulting flood of water that sustained the community and the livestock (Numbers 20:11).

Perhaps seeing this, Jesus, in a loud voice, linked himself to this water (John 7:37-38). His audience would have heard his speech as a messianic reference. It closely resembles Isaiah's invitation to God's banquet: "All you who are thirsty, come to the water" (Isaiah 55:1). Additionally, the disciples would have remembered Jesus referring to himself as living water in the drama with the Samaritan woman (John 4:13-15).

Jesus invited people to "believe" in him and drink (7:38). John used the Greek word for "believe" 86 times in his Gospel. It goes beyond an intellectual assent to doctrine. Rather, it conveys a sense of trusting, of having confidence in. Listening to Jesus with an open mind and heart will result in new life.

The Spirit would be poured out onto the disciples when the glorified, resurrected Christ breathed on them (20:22). The apostles would become examples of living water flowing abundantly into the early church.

The drama painted in today's passage invites each of us to join the crowd in asking, "Is Jesus the Christ?" Accepting his invitation to trust him, even with our lives, quenches the thirst in our hearts. The waters of life will become a living reality.

Indeed, who else has the words of eternal life (6:68)?

Lord, you call me out and offer me living water. Thank you for the chance to trust you in the daily scenes of my life. Amen.

Isaiah 25:6-10
A Banquet That Gives Hope

How do you find strength to deal with difficult times?

When you're going through a painful situation, it's difficult to focus on anything but the problem at hand. Taking a step back and seeing the problem within a broader timeframe can be helpful. Some of the pain may lose its sharpness from knowing that as days pass, new resources will be discovered and situations will change.

The prophet Isaiah wrote during a time of great suffering for Judah, the Southern Kingdom whose capitol was Jerusalem. The people lived in constant fear of conquest, and that fear was ultimately realized when the Babylonians destroyed their land in 586 BC.

In today's passage, as well as tomorrow's, the prophet encouraged the people by framing this suffering within a much larger context. Although it may have been difficult for them to see then, God was working to "swallow up" their hurt and "wipe tears from every face" (Isaiah 25:8).

Isaiah praised God's saving work in the opening verses of Chapter 25. Yahweh will overthrow tyrants and care for the poor, needy, and homeless. Then, in an image that would touch the hearts of a ravaged people, he describes a lavish banquet God will host in their honor. The fare will rival that of a royal feast. Its extravagance reflects God's heart. Moved by compassion, the Lord will spare no expense in welcoming the people to a land of renewed peace and prosperity.

Isaiah noted repeatedly that this future banquet will take place "on this mountain" (verses 6, 7, 10). This refers to Jerusalem, the city symbolic of God's calling of the Hebrew people and establishing them as a nation. The Lord's presence will return to the capitol. The disgrace they had felt at seemingly being abandoned will be replaced by joy in God's saving action.

This grace, though, will be extended beyond the Jews. The prophet noted that God will prepare the feast "for all peoples" (verse 6). The "shroud" (verse 7), which reflects the distance between the Lord's presence and humanity (Exodus 34:29-35), will be swallowed up. Israel will fulfill its destiny of being a light to the world (Isaiah 42:6).

This complete picture, with all people on earth gathered around the banquet table in Jerusalem, puts the difficulties of the present time into perspective. There's no way of knowing when such a vision will become a reality. Just because we hurt today, though, doesn't mean God isn't working to vanquish suffering and death, dry every tear, and make a home for all.

The vision of the future banquet proves God's work on behalf of those who suffer. Jesus, the one who invites all to his table, is the greatest proof.

Dear God, thank you for tirelessly working behind the scenes. Open my eyes, and I will praise your name forever! Amen.

Isaiah 55:1-3

A Different Type of Birthday Party

What does an invitation to a banquet reveal about God's heart?

Do you remember what it felt like to be invited to a birthday party when you were a child? What an honor it was that someone wanted to enjoy your company at an occasion that could be filled with food, games, and gifts!

Today's passage conveys an invitation that would be joyous and surprising to the Israelites. It was probably written toward the end of the Jews' exile in Babylon. The Persians would defeat the Babylonians (539 BC) and allow some of the Hebrews to return home. While this prospect encouraged the writer, he looked farther ahead and imagined a future time when the entire world will be united in a party around God's banquet table.

Our three verses today convey the excitement and passion behind the invitation to this feast. The Lord said "Listen!" twice (Isaiah 55:2, 3) and "Come!" three times (verses 1, 3). However, this invitation is not to an ordinary celebration.

First, there will be diversity and equality among the invited guests. Regardless of whether they have money, they will be invited. Oppression of the poor by the rich, including misconduct by those in power, had been a recurring sin in Israel (1:23; 3:14-15); but such oppression will eventually end because no one can buy a preferred place at God's table. Indeed, the impoverished themselves will have reserved seats: "The poor and the needy seek water, and there is none; their tongues are parched with thirst. I, the LORD, will respond to them; I, the God of Israel, won't abandon them" (41:17).

Second, guests will have to bring a gift of repentance. Isaiah 55:2 implies that people had misplaced their priorities, spending on things that didn't promote what was essential for life ("food"). Accepting the invitation will mean prioritizing God's desire for justice and righteousness. They will have to "seek the LORD while he can still be found" (verse 6).

God's passionate invitation to such a lavish banquet shows the Lord's faithfulness. Centuries before, Yahweh had promised David a dynasty where his people would live in peace (2 Samuel 7:9-11). Now, with all invited to the table, that promise will be fulfilled. As we saw in yesterday's text, a restored Jerusalem, David's city, will embody the new kingdom.

God's invitation in today's passage is an invitation to a different type of birthday party. It points to the dawn of an age when we will connect with God in a new, more intimate way. This will ultimately happen in a Bethlehem stable. When we celebrate Jesus' birth in a few weeks, we will be celebrating a love that will do anything possible to welcome us to the banquet table.

Lord, thank you for your relentless love. As I accept your invitation, I bring my life as a gift, yielded to you. Amen.

This winter, DAILY BIBLE STUDY *presents a series of readings supporting the theme "Engage." Readings come from the Old and New Testament texts. These daily readings, which prepare us for the 13 lessons in* Adult Bible Studies, *are written by Henry Brinton, Timothy Merrill, and Barbara Dick.*

Wait for It

Advent is a time of anticipation and waiting. These readings guide us to explore waiting as an important element in three episodes in Luke's telling of the Christmas story, in addition to other supporting biblical texts. They remind us that as much as we are called to wait for the Lord, Jesus Christ waits patiently for us.

Wonder

We are a busy people rushing from place to place and task to task as the hands of the clock chase each other around the dial. We get caught up in the mundane reality of ordinary life, and if we do not stop, we can so easily miss the extraordinary and sublime experience of entering into God's presence. These readings explore various ways human beings have experienced God's sublime glory and encourage us to become more sensitive to and aware of God's presence in the everydayness of our lives.

Show and Tell

These readings encourage us to explore various ways that we can participate with God through our actions. The word *work* and the doing of good deeds gets, unnecessarily, a bad rap in some Christian circles. When we read through the Old and New Testaments, we see that by engaging in life-giving activities, we join in the work to which God set our hands in the garden of Eden.